RESIDENTIAL INTERIORS

RESIDENTIAL INTERIORS

architectural & interior details

Charles Morris Mount

Architecture & Interior Design Library

An Imprint of

PBC INTERNATIONAL, INC. ✦ NEW YORK

Distributor to the book trade in the United States and Canada:

Rizzoli International Publications Inc.
300 Park Avenue South
New York, NY 10010

Distributor to the art trade in the United States and Canada:

PBC International, Inc.
One School Street
Glen Cove, NY 11542
1-800-527-2826
Fax 516-676-2738

Distributed throughout the rest of the world:

Hearst Books International
1350 Avenue of the Americas
New York, NY 10019

Library of Congress Cataloging-in-Publication Data

Mount, Charles Morris.
    Residential interiors, architectural and interior
    details / by Charles Morris Mount.
        p.   cm.
    Includes index.
    ISBN 0-86636-146-4
    1. Interior architecture.   2. Interior
    decoration.   3. Dwellings.   I. Title.
    NA2850.M6   1992
    729--dc20   91-45989
                                                     CIP

CAVEAT—Information in this text is believed accurate, and
will pose no problem for the student or casual reader.
However, the author was often constrained by information
contained in signed release forms, information that could
have been in error or not included at all. Any misinformation
(or lack of information) is the result of failure in these
attestations. The author has done whatever is possible to
insure accuracy.

For information about our audio products, write us at:
Newbridge Book Clubs, 3000 Cindel Drive, Delran, NJ 08370

Color separation, printing and binding by
Toppan Printing Co. (H.K.) Ltd. Hong Kong

Typography by
TypeLink, Inc.

10 9 8 7 6 5 4 3 2 1

Dedication

This book is dedicated to the memory of my brother, James Webster Mount—my guide to the design world; to my mother, Fannie Ruth Mount for her love and strength; and to Harold for constantly being my best critic and inspiration.

CHARLES MORRIS MOUNT
20th November, 1991
New York City

Table of Contents

Introduction

Interior design involves discipline and order. We all have this basic idea that we could be happy living in a beautifully designed interior space. Even primitive man wanted to control his own space. Decoration is synonymous with the high art of living well. Man's home is his castle and man's achievements were often measured in terms of his possessions and how he lived. This environment became his focal point—the center of domestic life.

When it was suggested to me to author a book on residential interiors, I thought to myself that this was a field that I am very familiar with, even though my main interest during my interior design career has been focused in the opposite direction...that of commercial design, mainly restaurant interiors. When I am asked to work with a client on a residential project, the scope of work usually concerns the "heart of the house"—the kitchen, but very often extends to the rest of the home as well.

I approached this assignment with a great deal of thought and contemplation about how to make the concepts of interior design come alive and how to keep the reader moving through the book. The term *global* does not necessarily refer to worldwide, but rather to the idea that these outstanding interior projects cover examples of contemporary design ideas found in our society.

In today's world, I find that there is little freedom of individual expression left, with one major exception... one's own environment, one's own living space. When I think of this simple concept, I realize how far interior design has come. In the modern sense, the time frame for this movement has been relatively short. The birth of modern design/decoration as a formal profession happened in the 17th century. Before this period, there was no division of labor among the arts of architecture, sculpture, painting and decoration. Artists designed a building's exterior and interior as well. Patrons controlled these artists and provided desirable commissions. The artists had an innate sense of scale, light and color. Paladio wrote his books on the rules and order of architecture. This was the beginning of interior design and decoration as we know it today.

There are so many ways of looking at interior design within a global perspective. We have many influences at hand...art, architecture, music, film, television, etc. Interior design has come to serve as an indicator of one's own education, taste, style, and socio-economic status. Interior design is the guide to understanding the personality of the client and the designer. The interior design reveals the socio-economic power as suggested by such early interior designers as Edith Wharton and Ogden Codman, Jr. in their book *Decoration of Houses*.

In sifting through the projects for this book, I have come upon another truth—that the design process is an editing process, a process of choosing and editing out in order to narrow the focus. As designers, we edit for our own as well as for our clients tastes. I feel that the strongest part of a room is the inherent intent of the architecture. Syrie Maugham was a great proponent of this idea, giving us the first "white room" in the 1930s. How very modern this idea seems today.

Changing lifestyles are always reflected in our architecture and interior design. Size and shapes of rooms change along with the function and decor. We are now seeing a blurring of the fine line between architecture and interior design/ decoration. Architects are creating more and more interiors and interior designers are becoming more and more influential as arbiters and contributors to the design of the exteriors of buildings. The many stylistic ideas and forms represented in these pages reveal a wide diversity of design and decoration concepts. This is a survey and is meant as a guide, a reflection of one person's conceptualization of the current world of interior design.

A&D Wejchert, Architects

DUBLIN HOUSE

Project Location
Dublin, Ireland
Design Firm
A&D Wejchert, Architects
Photographer
A&D Wejchert, Architects

THE HOUSE WAS DESIGNED for a professional couple with two children, to accommodate their lifestyle. Priority was given to family area: dining, conservatory and kitchen incorporated into one space. Adjoining is the library and audiovisual room. The layout took full advantage of the mature garden, the views toward distant hills and the southern orientation. All accommodations face south, and the conservatory creates an ideal extension of the garden into the house.

A limited budget and a narrow site influenced a compact layout, without a defined circulation area, with spaces flowing from one to another. Low maintenance and low energy costs were achieved by the use of self-finished natural materials (brick walls, clay paviors, pine ceilings and joinery) and by passive solar energy design. Most of the windows are positioned in the south facing wall; the north facing wall is heavily insulated and there are solar collector panels within the roof space. The conservatory adjoining the dining

Earthtone brickwork and woodwork add a great deal of warmth
and color to this cozy space. You
are always aware of the relationship of man to nature in this
house.

The texture and warmth of brick-work and woodwork contrasts nicely with the out-of-doors.

Nature is the real focus of this charming indoor–outdoor space. You are always aware of this relationship throughout the house – and vividly in this space. All the materials and finishes contribute to the totality of this space.

The giant climbing philodendron adds a tropical note. Texture and color are main design elements of this room.

area particularly suits the Irish climate, where sunshine in short intervals heats the highly absorbent clay paviors and brick walls, which in turn release the heat at night, creating a well tempered even environment.

Natural finishes of light colored brick and pine ceilings are supplemented with a bright red color for steel, light fittings and various accessories. This contrasts well with various shades of green seen through all windows of the house.

Even this kitchen gets into the act—an abundance of earthtone coloration and nicely contrasting textures, creates a practical, great-looking easily maintained space that is timeless.

This small study has its view onto the garden. You are always conscious of the indoors to out-of-doors relationship in this house.

There is warmth even in the stair.

HOUSE IN COUNTY CLARE

THIS HOUSE WAS DESIGNED for a woman who decided to settle in the west of Ireland, in County Clare. She previously lived in England, in an old stone cottage.

The house required accommodations for a single person, with space for visitors, and a large library.

Additionally, the house was to have some parts made of stone and had to be sympathetic to the surroundings.

The site is located on a slightly elevated hill, about 91 feet from Galway Bay, opening toward the Atlantic. It is on the outskirts of the Burren, an area famous for limestone rock formations. The most attractive views from the site are toward the Bay and Burren hills.

The basic decisions on the use of building materials followed careful analysis of the vernacular of that area:

- Limestone rubble wall around terrace, chimney and lower part of the house refers to the old traditions of simple rural structures of that area.
- Wet dash plaster and black roofing slate related to more recent housing traditions.

Solid loadbearing external walls with small window openings provide protection from extremely severe winds rushing from the Atlantic. The only one exceptional large glazed area in the entire facade is in the form of a bay window projected from

The warmth and textures of this house contribute to a simple, rich interior. This open space looking down into the sitting room from the library is dramatic and attention grabbing.

Project Location
Burren, County Clare, Ireland
Design Firm
A&D Wejchert, Architects
Photographer
A&D Wejchert, Architects

Texture and natural coloring is the design emphasis in this house. Natural stone is richly textured and enhances the rounded forms employed here.

the corner of the building. It was inspired by the similar element, although constructed in stone, in O'Brien Castle of Leamanch, originating from 1480 A.D. This "bay window" has a bench seat built along its three sides and offers spectacular panoramic views within the range of 270 degrees.

The house plan forms the letter "L." At ground floor level one wing contains the kitchen and the other bedrooms while the central part is for sitting and dining. The diagonal entrance leads toward the bay window, situated on the termination of the diagonal axis. The central part extends into the First Floor level, where the gallery offers access to extensive library bookshelves.

The lowest part of the house, as a result of a steep site profile, contains garage, utility room and boiler. All these three levels are interconnected by a circular spiral staircase, which is constructed entirely of stone, with individual slate steps set into the loadbearing limestone wall.

At the roof level, this staircase is terminated by a circular rooflight, admitting additional southern light into the central part of the house.

Anderson/Schwartz Architects

AN INTERIOR LANDSCAPE FOR A PRIVATE COLLECTION— FROM BAUHAUS TO MEMPHIS

Project Location
New York, New York, USA
Design Firm
Anderson/Schwartz Architects
Frederic Schwartz—Designer
Photographer
Todd Eberlee

T HE GRAND OLD APART-
ment buildings that rim
Central Park are minutes
away from some of the most
prestigious museums in the world.
But not all museum-quality objects
are on public display, many are
tucked away in the private residences
of nearby buildings. The design objective was to suggest a dialogue
with this important collection of
20th-Century furniture, including

originals and prototypes of notewor-
thy classics. The collection spans
periods from Bauhaus to Post-
modern, from de Stijl to Memphis
by such modern masters as Wright,
Breur, Rietveld, Eames, Aalto, Sottsass, Noguchi, Mies and Venturi.
This body of work was amassed by a
young connoisseur of the furniture
and decorative arts who began col-
lecting as a teenager. His choices
include tables, sofas, rugs, ceramics,

decorative art objects and TV cabinets as well as more than 40 chairs.

Transforming the prewar apartment into attractive areas of display for the client's diverse collection demanded a critical handling of a rich palette of materials, pattern, color and detail. Rather than a neutral museum-like setting, the collection and environment become active participants in an interior landscape of words, pattern, color and materials.

Writing on the walls, hardware, rugs, stenciling, tile patterns, leaded glass, new furniture, tile patterns, fabrics, lighting fixtures, accessories and decorative details were designed and assembled as a "garden of delights" to complement the rich mixture of furniture and decorative objects.

For example, the patterns of the new leaded glass doors combine patterns that refer to both the work of Wright and Sottsass. The stenciling in the library refers to the work of Mondrian and Rietveld. The colors and patterns in the dining area are a reference to both Venturi's early prototypes and Sottsass's early Memphis work.

The very small entry "Hall of the Giant Rose" in the apartment is expanded by the enormous scale of the flowers and the all over stenciled wall pattern. The roses refer to both the beauty and view of Central Park which is not yet seen at the entry. A suggestion that something very special is going on inside this apartment is revealed at the entry by the juxtaposed and multiple overlapping patterns. By removing the doors between the more public rooms but retaining the frames of the pre-war apartment, vistas are extended to other "interior landscapes."

At first sight nothing seems to resemble Eudoxia less than the design of that carpet, laid out in symmetrical motives whose patterns are repeated along straight and circular lines, interwoven with brilliantly colored spires, in a repetition that can be followed throughout the whole woof. But if you can pause and examine it carefully, you become convinced that each place in the carpet corresponds to a place in the city and all the things contained in the city are included in the design, arranged according to their true relationship, which escapes your eye distracted by the bustle, the throngs, the shoving. All of Eudoxia's confusion, the mules' braying, the lamp[...] smell is what is evident in the ind[...] you grasp; but the carpet pro[...]oint from which the city shows its [...] geometrical scheme implicit in [...]tail.

It is easy to get lo[...]hen you concentrate and s[...]ou recognize the street you were seeking in a crimson or indigo or magenta thread which, in a wide loop, brings you to the purple enclosure that is your real destination. Every inhabitant of Eudoxia compares the carpet's immobile order with his own image of the city, an anguish of his own, and each can find, concealed among the arabesques, an answer, the story of his life, the twists of fate.

Italo Calvino, *Invisible Cities*, pg. 96

The "Mondrian Oranges" room includes big vertical elements like the Skyscraper chair and surrounding stenciled trees which increase the scale and presence of the dining and kitchen area. Three very small rooms were converted into a kitchen and dining area. Chairs by noted architects Frank Lloyd Wright and Robert Venturi as well as the "Skyscraper Chair" by Frederic Schwartz command the view of an elongated custom dining table. A quote from Calvino surrounds the room connecting both ideas and the different elements of the design.

Barbara and Michael Orenstein Interiors
SUBURBAN RETREAT

This renovated Long Island house is beautifully sited with gardens and pool. Old trees and perennial plantings add distinction and charm to the entire project.

Project Location
Long Island, New York, USA
Design Firm
Barbara Orenstein Interiors
Photographer
Michael Mundy

THE CHARMING COUNTRY setting for this house and the interiors reflect the scale and sense of place. The layout is classic and open which is nicely reflected by the eclectic traditional mix of furnishings and use of color.

Upon entering the center hall, a staircase greets you, which leads to the second floor bedrooms. The main level is broken up into various living areas. The wood floor in the living room adds warmth and a sense of coziness. Two plump, neutral-toned sofas are carefully arranged by the fireplace to provide a comfortable conversational grouping,

anchored by a vibrant oriental area rug. A mixture of wood tones abound providing a pleasing melange of color. The coffee table is composed of a large piece of square glass on a mirrored base—an unusual, but fun addition.

The dining room contains an eclectic mixture of American country furnishings interspersed with European case goods. From the black wrought iron chandelier to the Persian area rug this is an inviting eating space. The large expanse bow window provides an abundance of

This is a classic New England type of residence. There is warmth and charm in the finishes and the arrangement of the furnishings.

natural light, and the absence of window treatments allows an unimpeded view of the beautifully maintained grounds surrounding the house.

The kitchen reveals the most personality from the designer and owner—the space is open with controlled, workable clutter that adds visual charm. This is a kitchen belonging to a serious cook; it contains a restaurant range and hood, a center island/work table, and an overhead industrial kitchen pot rack.

This is an interesting dining space—the tile floor with a large Persian carpet and the charming mix of American Country furnishings along with European furnishings. The large expanse of bow window brings in an abundance of natural light and a breathtaking view.

This is a kitchen for a serious cook—note the commercial cooking range, the pot rack and the center island. There is a charming confusion of old and new that works nicely.

This is a dramatic small guest toilet. The dark green walls expand this space, with the pedestal sink serving as a sculptural object.

This view of the kitchen gives you the chef's perspective. There is a dining table for four and a large country hutch displaying antique platters.

This view from the breakfast area in the large kitchen illustrates how much warmth comes from the wood floors. They are also very comfortable for the cook to stand on.

This view of the entry foyer illustrates how light-filled this country house is. The glow of the soft-colored walls and the warmth of the floor with its Persian carpet is enticing.

Bruce Bierman Design Inc.

WOODSBURG RESIDENCE

Project Location
Woodsburg, New York, USA
Design Firm
Bruce Bierman Design Inc.
Photographer
Jennifer Levy

THIS EXCEPTIONAL INTE-rior design by Bruce Bierman focuses on one word—neutrality. From the flooring, to the fixtures, to the cabinetry and woodworking, various beige tones predominate, yet never bore the viewer.

The kitchen is well planned and contains materials and finishes that are practical, yet elegant. Sleek granite countertops and back splash are in a lovely shade of brown to contrast with the neutrally-toned cabinetry. The lighting is designed with the cook in mind, as is the sculpturally beautiful center work island/breakfast bar. The shape of the dropped portion of the ceiling mirrors the shape of the center work island.

Neutral tones abound throughout the rest of the home, too. In the dining room, an absence of clutter and artwork provides a serene space for casual, as well as elegant dinner parties. Black accents are used here only on the dining table.

Black becomes a strong design feature and is nicely illustrated in the countertop and the two parallel black tile design featured on the wall.

This is a room Syrie Maugham would be happy to be dining in — white on white — beige on beige. The black line is sculptural and minimal.

This bedroom has a sensitive warmth and appeal—it's a friendly room and the colors are appealing and the furnishings comfortable and cozy.

The linear upholstered walls further add to the warmth and cozy aspect of this space.

The bathroom, also done in beige, utilizes black accents for interest. The vanity countertop and a parallel row of black tile encompassing the perimeter of the room break up and add visual interest to the neutral color expanse.

The master bedroom is rich, yet understated. The softness of the horizontal upholstered walls and the checked patterns of the bedspread and desk chair contrast nicely. The colors are harmonious and warm, yet subtle; the apricot and celadon green combination provides a nice balance. A media wall at the foot of the bed is concealed behind wood cabinetry that balances well with a lacquer closet wallsystem.

ALEXANDER JULIAN FARM

The exterior of this complex of buildings features multi-colored roof and patinated dormers.

FROM THE EXTERIOR OF this collection of farm buildings one senses that color and texture are important—from the patina and color on the roofs of these buildings to the texture and color applied to the shingled walls. The patina idea is carried throughout giving the complex artistic "pizzazz." The other design idea is how to create this "pizzazz" without spending an exorbitant amount of money. The budget was somewhat limited and creativity had to step in.

The interior of this complex has a wonderful collection of textures and finishes on the walls, kitchen cabinetry, and floors. The house is a riot of color, texture and finishes creating a whimsical and playful air. This is Alexander Julian's house—there is a certain relationship to the concept of his work, the multi-colored and textured walls all relate to his fabrics and clothing. The Julians plan to build a main house on this 37-acre complex. Therefore, this series of buildings would eventually become studios and guest houses.

Project Location
Connecticut, USA
Design Firm
Bruce Smith Designs
Photographer
Deborah K. O'Brien

Textured surface applications is a
big design feature of this kitchen.
This applied finish is contrasted
with natural twig and log design
elements and antique furnishings.

BREAD

This charming still life is of garlic heads in a recessed niche in the kitchen. The cabinetry is applied surface decoration.

The wood walls have been scraped down and part of the old color paint left in place. The Daniel Mack chair works beautifully and sculpturally here.

Natural materials such as twigs and logs were utilized as main design elements. Common materials such as burlap, muslin, plaster of Paris, white glue and paint were utilized to create the various textures and colors in this "reclothed" house. To paint the roofs, for example, Bruce Smith poured on gallons of deck paint. Assistants then hosed the roof with water. Different shades of blue, green, white and dark purple were utilized to achieve the final result: a painted roof that from a distance resembles beautifully aged copper.

This is a fun stairwell—the natural tree form and the pots of flowering plants, with the warmth of the natural wood treads works well with the linen white walls.

Clodagh

ARTIST'S/COLLECTOR'S RESIDENCE

THIS RESIDENCE IS FOR AN artist/collector; designer Clodagh has had a creative good time here. This design utilizes a myriad of decorative elements—color, texture, graphics, lighting. This is a statement not only for the client but also for the designer—"Take a look and don't be afraid to express yourself." This is bare-chested, exuberant design.

Project Location
New York, New York, USA
Designer
Clodagh
Architect
Robert Pierpont
Photographer
Daniel Aubry

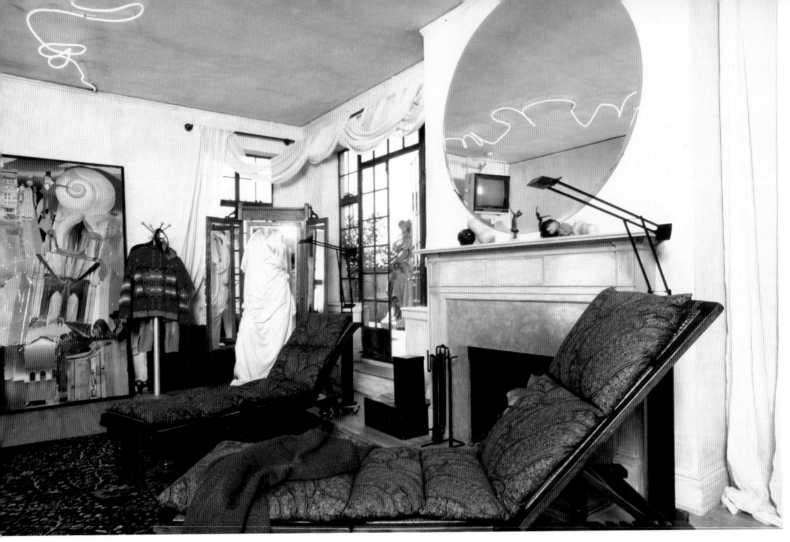

The living room with its quizzical neon flitting across the ceiling and two special chaise lounges arranged in front of the fireplace makes a strong, dramatic statement. The sculptural draping in front of the pier mirror and the drapes at the corner windows work together and somehow mimic the neon patterns on the ceiling. The television hanging from the ceiling further adds to the eccentric design. The bedroom, with its crazy hat collection, is another expression of fun. Even paintings of hats adorn the walls. The out-of-doors room is a riot of color and texture. The oeil d'beouf is unexpected and frames the spatial view beyond.

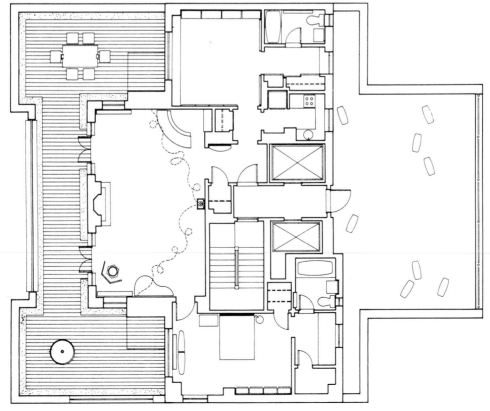

TERRACE APARTMENT

Project Location
New York, New York, USA
Designer
Clodagh
Architect
Robert Pierpont
Photographer
Daniel Aubry

THE HANDLE ON THE front door gives it away: there is a special designed space just behind the door. The door is a textual/colorful finish in varying antiqued hues. The undulating entrance hall makes its own bold statement through its shape and the artwork displayed on its wall. The lighting enhances the volume of the space, as well as the art—it appears as if the art is growing out of the walls and becoming a part of the whole design statement.

The wall color creates a seemingly endless background, which enhances the flow and movement of spaces. This creates a charming confusion between indoors and out-of-doors. The colors seem to meld into each other and reinforce each other.

The overall architecture underscores the design statement and works with it in a wonderful way. An important note is the furnishings; they were purposefully designed to take a "back seat" to the architecture, yet they enhance the interior design and play up the varying architectural detailings.

The handle to the front door
gives the first impression—there
is something very special inside
this door. Here you witness the
commanding foyer/art gallery.
The undulating space pulls one
into the residence.

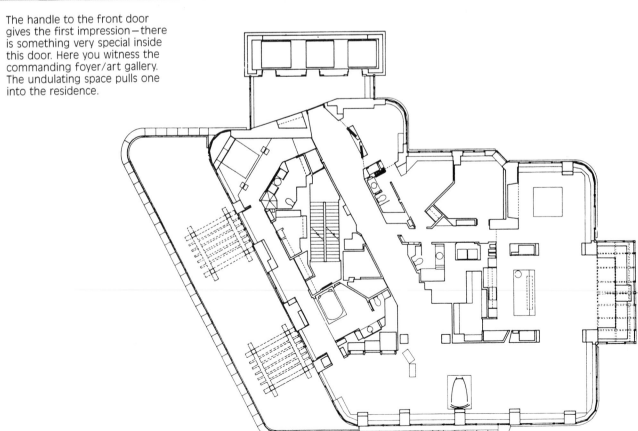

The architecture becomes the important design element of this entire project—the wonderful angled forms, the colors, the light, and air of this space all work together to create a special ambience.

The open kitchen with its counter and the dining area with its cityscape view all add-up to an intriguing rich design solution. Soft subtle colorings seem to underline and underscore the architectural statement.

This master bath is just that—masterful and grand. The marble adds a warmth and richness that few other materials can. The soft pink walls and ceiling further add warmth and richness to this design solution.

The guest bathroom has its own richness—its copper clad vanity and towel bars. There is natural slate in the tub/shower enclosure.

Damga Design Inc.

NEW JERSEY APARTMENT

Project Location
Union City, New Jersey, USA
Design Firm
Damga Design Inc.
Charles Damga, Vazgen Houssian — Design Team
Photographer
Peter Paige

THE PRIMARY GOAL OF THE design was to capitalize on the sweeping views of Manhattan by pulling down the exterior walls and expanding the living area into the long gently curved terrace. The whole enterprise was also to be accomplished with an eye toward destroying any semblance the space had to its former status—a typical two-bedroom highrise apartment.

The long terrace was eliminated and replaced by a floor-to-ceiling curved window wall. At each end of the window wall a large 8′ by 8′ expanse of mirror was set perpendicular to the windows. These mirrors continue the reflection of the curving windows, but are slightly skew to the living space. The result was dramatic. The side walls seem to disappear into an endless reflection of the curving windows.

The second bedroom, an infrequent guest room and cramped home studio with no view, was removed next. Now open to the big room, a two-step high platform was erected in the same approximate area. Topped by a long angled white countertop, this space has a commanding view (over the lounge seating in front of it) of the golden city skyline at dusk. The counter, over 13 feet long, doubles as a work space for design and a bar/buffet ledge for entertaining. Extensive use of long, uninterrupted diagonals with open site lines such as in this counter give the entire space a larger visual impression.

In the living area the two heat pumps, formerly located on the exterior wall, were disconnected, joined and relocated off to a side wall. They were hidden by an unusual enclosure. Stainless steel rods, spaced ½ inch apart, were spread lengthwise over the entire top of the 10′ long heat pump expanse serving as an unusually beautiful surface

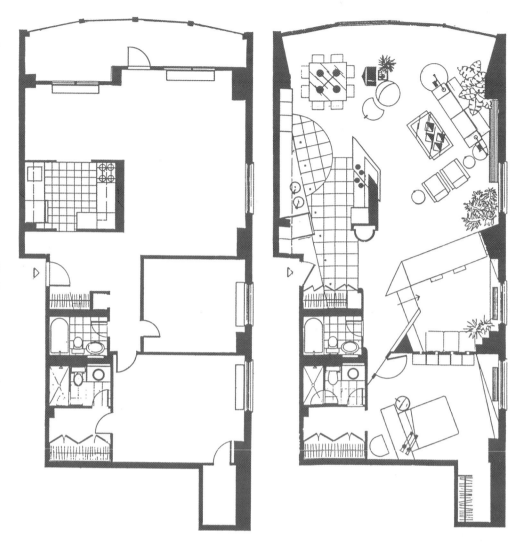

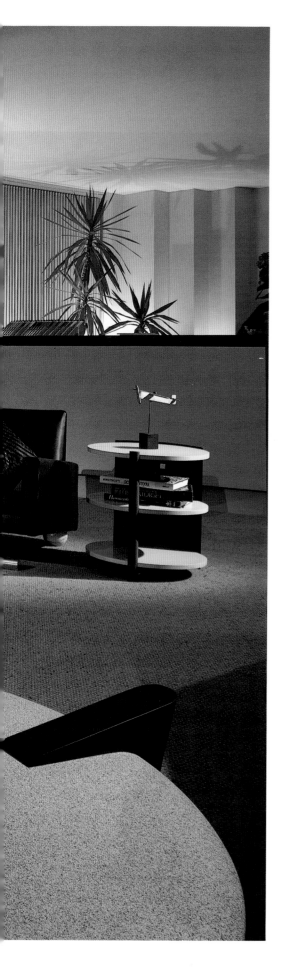

while eliminating the need for a separate grill. All living room furnishings were chosen for their slim, low projection and all are on legs to allow light from the windows to pass through them. Each is a custom piece from the designers' new furniture collection (see ID April 90 issue) except for the B & B sofa. The furniture is angled away from the walls, in a diagonal arrangement to keep the spatial definition of the room pure and the view unobstructed. A custom round swiveling chair, large enough to seat two people nested in a crescent-shaped side table near the windows as the favored perch of the owner.

The coffee table comprises two pieces of glass suspended over four tetrahedrons of stainless steel set on edge. The weight and smoothness of the glass combine to create a partial vacuum that allows the top glass to slide surprisingly easily. Thus, the three by five foot top can expand to four by seven foot.

The kitchen, formerly open only to the dining room, was the next space to be liberated. All walls that could possibly be taken down were. A five-foot wall remained around which a richly-faceted island was constructed. Put together with many discretely different elements the island comes together as a valid sculptural whole, revealing surprising views as one walks its perimeter. This innovative cooking center serves many functions. At the end nearest the entry is a full-height cylindrical glassware cabinet whose circularity complements the many diagonal elements of the room. Next to this cabinet is a vertically stacked oven cabinet, housing, from top to bottom, a microwave, two convection ovens and a pot drawer. All hardware was removed and redesigned and all faces replaced by black glass doors. An adjacent stainless steel drawer unit is punctuated by electric burners. The burners were individually liberated from their base component and rewired. Two of the

burners were set into this top. The two other burners were set into the last component—a cobalt blue diamond-shaped steel polygon. This wedge shaped polygon, seemingly thrust into the island, is four inches higher than the stainless steel drawer unit in order to house the square vent holes of the concealed downdraft fan. It also houses the television and VCR on the side facing the living area. Two angular glass shelves and a soffit, with halogen recessed lights, float above,

reinforcing the thrust of the blue polygon.

The opposite wall of the kitchen area is dominated by a forty-foot expanse of black lacquered upper cabinets. It is followed below by a line of lower cabinets topped by a stainless steel countertop. One third of the way down, the whole lower counter pivots twenty-two-and-a-half degrees into the room as if pulled out from an invisible hinge. This gesture enables the two stainless steel sinks, each with its' own single lever faucet, to be utilized with the necessary headroom. The end of this lever arm counter is weighted with a refrigerator that fully delineates the pivoting gesture. The space resulting behind the refrigerator is not lost, however; it can be accessed by a sliding panel on its exposed side.

The floor treatment, neutral light-grey carpeting, was interrupted in the kitchen by two bold geometric areas of metallic grey tiles. Formed with impact in mind, one, a large circle; and the other, a slicing diagonal; explicitly show the generating forces of the room design. The tile areas, perceptably different in hue, are inlaid with a line of two-inch square solid brass inlays.

The original privacy wall to the bedroom is bifurcated by a skew yellow wall with a meticulously flush door. It slopes down into the studio area on one side and it stops ten

inches shy of the bathroom wall on the other. At this point a wall-height section of clear glass is inserted to close the gap. This strange wall acts as a two-way funnel either to the raised studio or the bedroom. The privacy wall of the bedroom is punctured by four 4½″ square holes at eye level allowing peephole views into the main space and shafts of the morning light to penetrate the bedroom. Both bathrooms were renovated in the designer's favored method-large white tiles, mirror, and white fixtures.

Wall treatments are industrial zolatone; lavendar grey in the kitchen, and a faint pastel yellow in the rest of the apartment. Track lighting is halogen with concealed remote transformers. All other lighting is quartz or low voltage halogen, all of which can be controlled by hand-held remotes with dimmers.

GEOMETRIC FORMS

THE DESIGN CONCEPT BE-
hind this New York high-rise
apartment is to break up the
rectangular nature of the
space through the use of color and
geometric forms both on the walls
and the floors without resorting to
any structural changes. A custom
carpet runs throughout with insets of
triangles, circles, squares, and diagonals bisecting rooms, changing
colors, playfully flowing through the
space. Wall treatments of varying
textures range from soothing pastels
to brilliant saturated blues and vio-
lets. Large geometric mirrors were
strategically placed to expand con-
fining, narrow rooms.

The long opposite walls of the
narrow living and dining area
(35′ × 12′) are painted dramatically
different colors, thereby disconnect-
ing them and widening the space
visually. On one side, the pale blue
faux-finish connects with the sim-
ilarly-hued carpeting, while on the
other an intense violet and cobalt
blue (bisected by a low molding) de-
liberately exaggerates the extreme
length of the room. The living space

Project Location
New York, New York, USA
Design Firm
Damga Design Inc.
Charles Damga, Coco Roule,
Rob Harrison — Design Team
Photographer
Peter Paige

is composed with oversized seating set away from the walls at acute angles to defy the rectilinearity of the room. The custom dining table is made of an inverted brushed steel tetrahedron which hovers an inch above the floor floating in a triangular open frame. The top is blue pearl granite. Brushed brass window ledges with sleek long angles or curves mimic the floor patterns. Clean simple lighting was achieved through the use of black low voltage track lighting and Artemide's new Zen lamp.

The den colors are more somber shades of grey and lavender. A bar and media cabinet, finished in an anthracite grey laminate, with a blue pearl granite top, and frosted glass shelves with built-in undercounter lights is set into one wall.

The bedroom is mirrored at one end and a textured midnight blue gives the impression that there are no corners or walls, evoking a sense of infinity. A media cabinet is cut into the wall opposite the B&B Italia bed. Upholstered in dark blue suede, this king-size bed has adjustable, rotating side tables and back supports.

The successful play of forms, color, and space transform this apartment from a tiresome box, into a delightful sensory experience.

WEST END AVENUE RENOVATION

This project reflects a close working relationship between the designer and his client—there was close and careful scrutiny of materials, finishes, and details. This is an on-going project and this design collaboration is going on five years and both are still on friendly terms.

Project Location
New York, New York, USA
Design Firm
Damga Design Inc.
Charles Damga, Coco Roule,
Rob Harrison—Design Team
Photographer
Peter Paige

THE DESIGNER WORKED closely with the client to make sure that no details remained unresolved, and that the contractor delivered in the end. This project was a five-year odyssey that both designer and client endured, and the final design, like their relationship, is strong.

The living room is a large space, with the main seating area defined by a custom designed carpet. The seating surrounds an oversized verde green marble coffee table. The lighting in this room is subdued and highlights artwork, plants and architectural details.

Each room is an exciting melange of architectural details, artistic finishes and eclectic furnishings. The dining room has a faux marbre molding that points up the built-in marble sideboard. The faux marbre molding surrounding the window creates the illusion of a painting, framing the window treatment, thus providing a dramatic flair.

This living room is a large space—
the main seating area is defined
by a large custom design carpet.
The seating centers around a
large verde green marble coffee
table and beyond one can see
into the dining room. Lighting focuses on art works.

This is a view of the entrance foyer. The arch welcomes guests into this apartment. There is a nice contrast between new and old—the architecture and decoration of the apartment with the furnishings and the colors.

The master bedroom is lavish and indulgent—the beautifully proportioned vaulted ceiling with its trompe l'oeil and the highly detailed, fine cabinetry work together to convey an overall impression of sophistication. Furnishings and art accessories further promote the opulent, elegant air. Here, as in the rest of this residence, the lighting design is key to the effectiveness of the overall design statement.

This is a room of grand proportions and grand furnishings. The scale is quite dramatic. The custom-designed carpet with the custom-fabricated sideboard adds to this sense of space. The lighting valance and the window surrounds are faux finish marble.

The custom carpet creates a strong design statement in this space. Black forms on a soft mauve background create an interesting visual and graphic contrast.

This painting of a cherub adds to the atmosphere of this dining room. The painting is illuminated by light fixtures concealed behind the faux marble valance.

This is a bedroom for the client's daughter and is very charming and feminine. There is toy storage underneath the bed unit.

This is a little boy's room and says so instantly. The bold color statement and the fun architectural elements along with the raised platform create an appropriately interesting space for a boy.

This is an unusual and interesting
master bedroom—the vaulted
ceiling with its faux clouds—the
large overscaled furnishings and
custom cabinetry all make for a
rich design statement. The walls
are a painted textured finish and
one perceives a certain richness
from the wood finishes on the
cabinetry.

D'Aquino Humphreys Interiors

RESIDENCE AT WASHINGTON COURT

This is a rarity in New York City—
an apartment with a garden! This
is a very simple, yet complex out-
of-doors space—long and narrow.
The finishes are appropriate:
stone flooring, teak furnishings
and lots of plantings.

This is a nicely-proportioned room—generous architectural moldings, wainscot, and fireplace surround. The room gives off a natural glow, thanks to lots of natural light from skylights and large windows.

OLD WORLD ELEGANCE abounds in this New York apartment designed by D'Aquino Humphreys Interiors. Numerous architectural detailings—from the intricate moldings, to the skylights, to the red marble fireplace surround, to the wainscotting, give this living room flair and panache. Finely

Project Location
New York, New York, USA
Design Firm
Geordi Humphreys and Carl D'Aquino
of D'Aquino Humphreys Interiors
Photographer
Guy Lindsay

The rich red marble adds a great deal of design interest to the fireplace surround. The gold color on the andirons is picked up in the wainscotting and furnishings.

finished exposed wood flooring contrasts nicely with European style furnishings. Monumental drapery/window surrounds command attention and further enhance the beauty of this design.

The garden is long and narrow, so the design was kept simple and unencumbered. Stone flooring, teak furnishings and an abundance of plantings are thoughtfully used to impart a tranquil feeling.

The color palette for this room is sensitive and unusual. The unusual Celadon green walls are further echoed in the fabrics and the antique paneled screen.

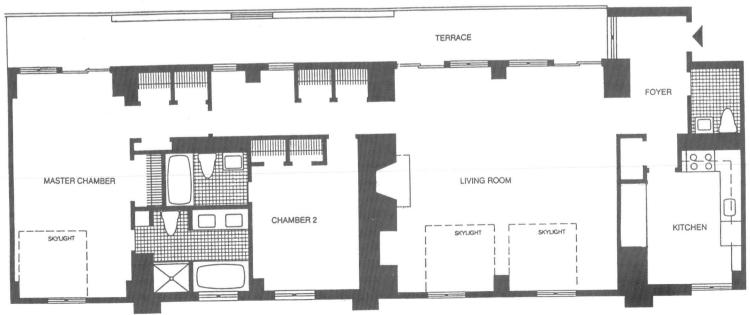

DuBay & Maire Designs

CLASSICAL COMFORT

THIS CHICAGO APARTMENT is a symphony in cream and beige. The furnishings are traditional and provide a good, strong base for the overall look of this residence. The cream-colored walls provide a unifying backdrop for the art and furnishings. The materials and finishes work well together, with the whole being greater than the sum of its parts. Modern track lighting provides overall illumination, while ambient lighting is provided by various floor lamps and torchieres.

The kitchen boasts a free-hanging, stainless steel hood, Korian® countertops, and simple cabinetry in a pleasing off-white shade. The exposed pine flooring adds a touch of color and warmth to the space and unifies the living spaces.

This project has very simple classical lines—from the overstuffed sofas to the tapestries, carpets, and oriental screens.

Project Location
Chicago, Illinois, USA
Design Firm
DuBay & Maire Designs
Photographer
Tony Soluri

The gently curving wall in this room is custom fitted with a velour covered seating unit. Hassocks add to the comfort level. The black background of the needlepoint rug brings in a pleasing decorative element to the space.

There is a small table in the living area of this apartment for card games or a small dinner party. The lighting in this area is sufficient and pleasing.

This is a generous kitchen for a city apartment. This space features a center work island with a cooktop and a stainless steel hood and pot rack. Botanical prints add a decorative touch to this clean space.

This bedroom is very soft, visually. The color and lighting both contribute to the room's soft glow and visual comfort image. The master bedroom focuses on a majestic four poster bed, and again we see a soft simple color solution. The lighting adds another layer onto the design solution.

Gwathmey Siegel & Associates Architects

SHELBURNE FARMS

THE SITE IS A TWELVE acre, wooded, peninsula on Lake Champlain, with panoramic views north and west across and down the Lake to the Adirondack Mountains.

The design parti is both programmatic and site specific, in that it separates the guest and children's areas from the main house. These elements are organized along an "arcade/spine" and are interconnected visually through a series of courtyard spaces and a single pitched roof.

Each of the "house" facades is articulated by a fireplace/chimney object and interconnected across the courtyards by a continuous horizontal cross beam/scupper element. The organization affords varying lake views from every habitable space, while maintaining a sense of individual identity and intimacy.

Project Location
Shelburne, Vermont, USA
Design Firm
Gwathmey Siegel & Associates Architects
Paul Aferiat — Associate in Charge
Photographer
Richard Bryant

The play of light and shadow among the architectural forms is pleasing, interesting and visually exciting.

The articulated facade with its varying roof structures becomes very playful and fun. Color is an important design element in this house and the red contrasts well with the coolness of the other finishes.

This is a beautiful facade—the
starkness of the contemporary
architecture with its glass block
and red elements contrasted with
the field stone wall.

A linear spacial sequence is initiated at the auto court with the entry at the south end of the spine. One passes between the garage and the stair to the children's "bunk house," which is the second floor; to the lakeside opening in the arcade, accessing the pool terrace, past the caretaker's apartment, to the garden/landscape opening in the arcade with the two "guest house" entrances opposite, arriving at the north and entry to the "main house."

This residence is both universal and specific. It creates a sense of place, through the manipulation of architecturally defined outdoor spaces, circulation, site engagement and massing variation. It is conceived as both a single building that addresses the scale of the site and lake, and as an assemblage of distinct objects, articulated by their roof forms, and courtyards.

Water becomes a beautiful design element in this photo. Contrast, light and shadow are all evident.

The fireplace becomes one with the view beyond. The glass block creates a diamond diadem surround for the fireplace.

Spatial volumes reflect the architectural intent. These are great rooms in scale and proportion, and are truly exciting, living spaces.

This space has a charming shape—it reflects what is happening on the exterior. The natural light enhances its volume.

The fireplace is a beautiful sculptural element within this room.

Natural northern light is the best for a painter's studio. This room has majestic proportions and warm, simple finishes.

EASTERN LONG ISLAND GET AWAY

THE PROGRAM INCLUDED A main house, pool, tennis court, and caretaker's house with guest and garage facilities on a four acre ocean-front site. The total integration of building and landscape design, each reinforcing the object/space, sequence/circulation dynamics and revelations, was primary to the overall composition.

Project Location
East Hampton, New York, USA
Design Firm
Gwathmey Siegel & Associates Architects
Gustav Rosenlof—Associate in Charge
Joan Jasper—Project Architect
Photographers
Stephen Brooke
Eduard Heuber

This is a tremendously proportioned room—the fireplace becomes the focus of the space and a main design feature. Color emphasizes the chimney forms and adds further interest.

The site sequence is asymmetrical and layered in both the north-south and east-west axis. The driveway, bound by a row of bald cyprus trees on the west and a double hedge on the east, is axial to the south and views the Atlantic Ocean through a pear tree courtyard at its end. The initial architectural revelation begins with the caretaker's structure, followed sequentially by the tennis court, "gate house" which is a storage mechanical structure, and entry court. The main house presents a three story facade to the north, which both anchors the site, establishes a wall, and implies a gate to the dune and ocean beyond. The two story "brise-soliel" framed facade presents itself as an articulated, dynamic counterpoint.

Color is an important design element of this structure—warm umbrian colors are used throughout the entire house. The walls glow with warm Tuscan colors. The floor changes pattern and color and is set off with a black feature strip.

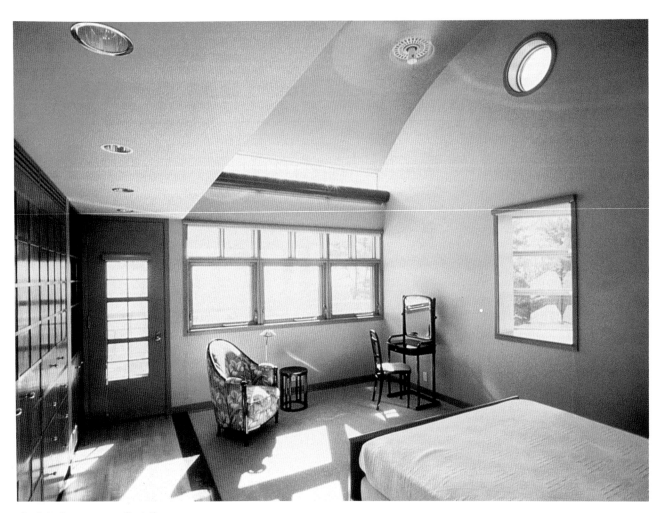

The interior spaces reflect the exterior architecture—this bedroom has a soaring vaulted ceiling and the walls have a warm soft glow. There is abundant natural light from skylights and interestingly shaped windows.

The fireplace is the obvious focal point of this room, but you are always aware of the majestic Atlantic Ocean just beyond the house. The wood floor is a rich color done in a herringbone pattern.

The main entry/site stair is scaled to the garden and the ocean, defining the berm, which establishes the site level change from the lawn to the dune. The design of this residence engenders the composition with the appropriate sense of scale and anticipation, and attempts to exploit the natural site variations, both physical and perceptual, extend the "modern vernacular" while referring to precedents embodied in the major "dune" house of the 1920's and 1930's.

Guest bedrooms are almost spartan in design yet the finishes are in keeping with the rest of this house. The furnishings have an Arts and Crafts Movement spirit.

Haverson/Rockwell Architects, PC

ARCHITECT'S APARTMENT

This unusual temple facade welcomes one into a penthouse apartment. This new structure sits atop a New York City apartment tower.

THIS CITY AERIE IS AN AP-propriate space for an architect. There are views of almost every conceivable type of architecture, even though most of it is on the roof tops of buildings. This classical facade set on top of a '20s apartment house in New York City has its own environment and roof top terrain. The space beyond the facade is simple and well designed. The materials and finishes are exemplary and the entire scheme works well. The rooms are beautifully proportioned; the ceiling heights are generous but not intimidating; additionally, it's coved and illuminated. The dining room with its classic door and windows, is further enhanced with the richness of cherry floors and frames. The red and white webbing on the Shaker chairs adds geometric interest. The soft apricot color in the ceiling cove adds warmth to this space. The other public spaces are comfortable and casual in style and furnishings. The sisal type flooring in the living room is a textural contrast to the tile floor.

Project Location
New York, New York, USA
Design Firm
Haverson/Rockwell Architects, P.C.
Photographer
Paul Warchol

This galley kitchen is small but extremely functional. Wood cabinetry adds warmth; the wood floor is comfortable and easy to maintain.

The dining room has windows on three sides and adds a nice touch to this well-proportioned room. The coved ceiling with its special recessed lighting makes this a special room for dining.

This very simple living space is rich in color, texture and architectural detail. Color is rich, yet soft and inviting. There is an abundance of natural light and the architects designed a lighting system that is functional yet unobstrusive.

The tile pattern in the master bathroom recalls tile work of the early 1900s. The terrazzo counter-top is playful and fun, yet very practical and easy to maintain.

The master bedroom has a bed platform with storage under-neath. The walls are painted in a pink tone, and the pillows on the bed recall early American quilt patterns.

Huberman Designs

THE CASTLE ON LONG ISLAND

THIS DESIGNER SHOWCASE House is very special architecturally and decoratively. It is rich and opulent. The library recalls the era of J.P. Morgan and his cronies; the richness of these rooms is worthy of the period and the furnishings are an appropriate eclectic mix of many styles. This room is majestically proportioned and the architectural detail of the woodwork is wonderful. The book cases are appropriately restrained, yet add to the overall richness of the space. The exterior recalls the Chateaux of France, Louis the XV, and earlier periods of architecture and design.

Project Location
Cold Spring Harbor, New York, USA
Design Firm
Huberman Designs
Photographer
Norman McGrath

This is a tremendous room in one of the grand old estates on Long Island. The woodwork is beautifully detailed and executed. The furnishings are large scaled for this room and are appropriate. The fireplace surround is marble and the Persian carpets are what one would expect for these grand spaces.

This is a view of the main entrance foyer with its horseshoe staircase. This is a room of grand scale and proportions and reflects the opulence of days past.

This ballroom is simple yet grand. The chandeliers and the wall sconces are all gold, crystal and glitter. The walls have a soft lively color scheme and the hardwood floors are original.

This is the State Dining Room, and a room for large dinner parties with chamber music. The floors are stained darker in this space, while the walls are several shades of cream.

This is a view of the ballroom from the opposite end. These spaces are magnificently proportioned and finished. The moldings are scaled to the room.

Joan Halperin
Interior Design
PARK AVENUE RENOVATION

The background here is what's important—let the art work stand out. The lighting is designed to highlight the art and the space is beautiful, functional, and livable.

THIS RENOVATION IS SIMPLE yet effective—it makes use of straight forward thinking "let the background stay in the background and let the art do the talking." The furnishings and the art are integral along with the lighting and simple architectural detailing.

The dining room is charming with its bookcase-lined walls. The chandelier is the most important element within the space and is a wonderful sculptural contrast to the art and the red walls. The living room has a light open feeling and the space feels expansive. The areas flow easily into each other creating an open, airy floor plan.

Project Location
New York, New York, USA
Design Firm
Joan Halperin Interior Design
Photographer
Darwin K. Davidson

This is an art gallery for contemporary art and the designer has concentrated on setting-up an appropriate background and lighting scheme for the display of this art.

This is a cozy little den with some Matisse Jazz prints. The patterned wallpaper picks-up on designs found in the prints.

This red dining room recalls Georgian design ideas—the Russian chandelier and the Georgian furnishings certainly add to this design idea, but then you notice the light bleached wood floor and the modern art.

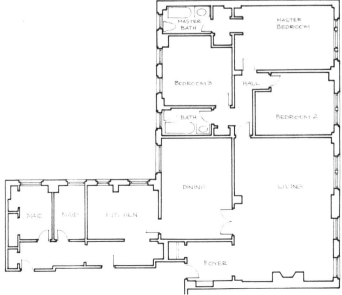

Before

The corridor to the master bedroom becomes a gallery space for
the display of a beautiful light box
and small framed prints.

The master bathroom is simple in
its all-white color solution. All-
white bathrooms are rare these
days. This bathroom has a very
beautiful finish and the brass
touches add richness.

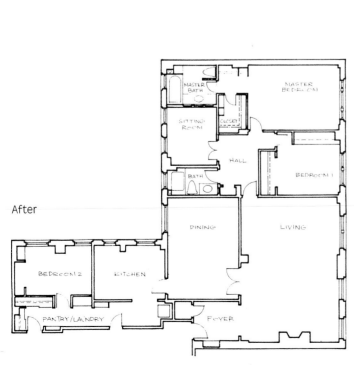

After

The Joseph Boggs Studio / Architects

URBAN TOWNHOUSE

A VILLA CONCEPT WAS utilized for this townhouse built in an urban residential community located on a third of an acre of commercial waterfront property. The topography is level with a sparse planting of trees.

The villa concept required inserting into the urban context a progressive, linear organization of building volumes including a pool house, caretaker house and associated garages. The main house offers a ground level entry with a small office and a two-car garage. The upper two levels constitute the main living area and contain two bedrooms and a den/guest room.

The seemingly freestanding frontal facade is of masonry. The verticality of the facade responds to the emphasis of height in respect to width required in the plan organization. The parti of open and closed spaces are made more mysterious by the surrounding wall resembling a fortification of the site, while light and air penetrate the pool enclosure and the associated private outdoor spaces.

The eastern facade at dusk.

The western facade at dusk.

Project Location
Annapolis, Maryland, USA
Architectural Firm
The Joseph Boggs Studio/Architects—
Joseph Boggs, Design Principal
Michael Callison, Project Architect
Interior Designer
Celeste Hart Interior Design
Photographer
Maxwell Mackenzie

The geometric rigor of the house both in elevation, plan and section respond to a 45-degree structural element of macro/micro proportions. This "structural" language unifies the three-dimensional aspects of the house plans and continues on surface planes throughout the pool house. Geometric order is further supplemented by the 10-degree vertical sculptural columns. This splayed geometry is further used in the pool bridge and the caretaker's house ceiling.

Architectural structure pieces are finished in gloss white for emphasis.

Living spaces smoothly flow into each other creating an open feel.

The frontal facade is composed predominantly of masonry.

The view from the master bedroom on the third level.

Architectural elements enhance
the verticality of this villa
townhouse.

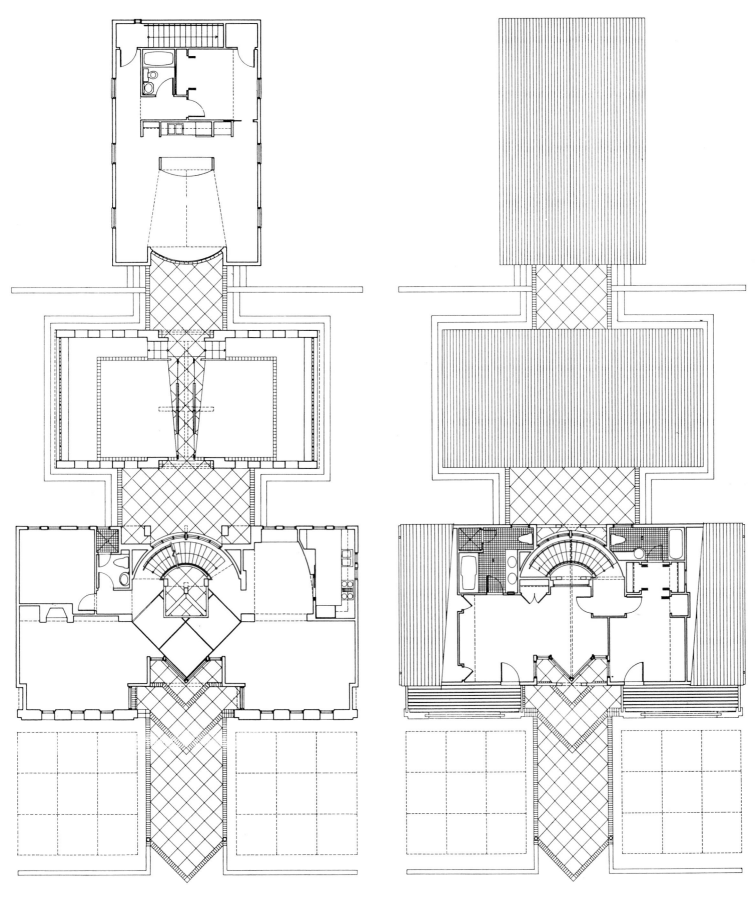

SECOND FLOOR PLAN

THIRD FLOOR PLAN

A SOUTHERN VILLA

Project Location
Great Falls, Virginia, USA
Design Firm
The Joseph Boggs Studio/Architects
Joseph Boggs, A.I.A. – Principal
Project Architect
Michael Callison
Photographer
Maxwell Mackenzie

A THREE-ACRE ROLLING parcel with panoramic wooded vistas served as the basis for this house, with no adjacent houses within visibility.

The designer's goal was to provide a residence with guest quarters and a garage of approximately 6,500 heated square feet. A special requirement was to house an international furniture collection and other antiquities.

An architectural language of forms was derived from Tuscany imagery to provide the scale and villa forms which seemed appropriate to this client's background and cultural interest. The house became a composition of spaces that allowed the light and shadow to interplay throughout the structure. A major cylindrical entry element anchored the house allowing wings to emanate in two directions to create inside-outside spaces. The entrance foyer also contains a second story viewing gallery and a dramatic ceiling with

The Northern facade of the residence.

The entrance foyer provides an impactful statement to the "villa" theme. The second story viewing gallery is visible from the foyer.

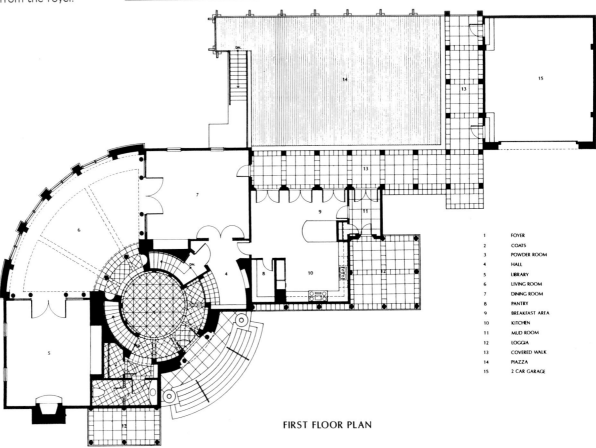

1	FOYER
2	COATS
3	POWDER ROOM
4	HALL
5	LIBRARY
6	LIVING ROOM
7	DINING ROOM
8	PANTRY
9	BREAKFAST AREA
10	KITCHEN
11	MUD ROOM
12	LOGGIA
13	COVERED WALK
14	PIAZZA
15	2 CAR GARAGE

FIRST FLOOR PLAN

The master bathroom utilizes
glass block to provide privacy, yet
allows natural light to filter into
the bedroom.

An abundance of natural light,
softly curving walls, and a
plethora of traditionally styled
antique furniture provides a
tranquil air in the master
bedroom.

A view indoors from the outside
terrace.

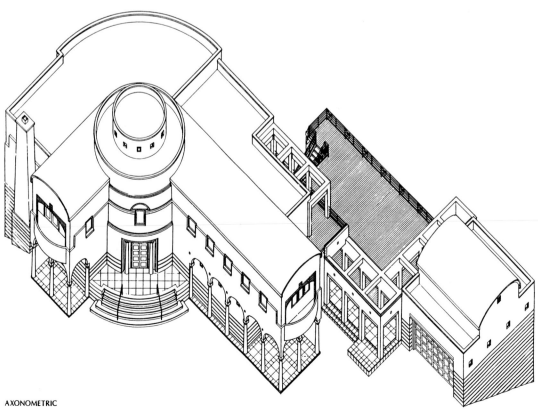

AXONOMETRIC

Kevin Walz Design

SHELTER ISLAND VICTORIAN HOME

The front porch and facade convey the Victorian ambience one
associates with Shelter Island.
But, just beyond these double
doors a special treat awaits.

Project Location
Shelter Island, New York, USA
Design Firm
Kevin Walz Design
Kevin Walz — Principal
Martin Sosa — Project Manager
Photographer
Barbra Walz

This living room is a charming blend of Victorian detail and contemporary furnishings. There are wonderful folk art rugs and very casual window treatments. This is a vacation home and the spirit of the place says "let's have fun."

THIS CHARMING RENOVATION/restoration is of a 108-year-old Victorian beach house. The goal was to open up the small Victorian spaces into more airy, light-filled rooms. From the front door to the spacious interior, the detailing of the old style was maintained, and the new was brought into the design context as an underlying, grace note. The old style wainscot was maintained in the kitchen and pantry along with the glass-fronted cabinets. There is a fun and creative theme throughout this project. This project is a story of contrasts, from the slick contemporary to the Victorian. Objects are contemporary, yet maintain the "Victorian" ideal. The juxtaposition of old with new creates an interior design that is sophisticated, yet comfortable.

There are collections of family photographs grouped together on walls. Simplicity is the password here.

The dining room is where it all happens—large family get-togethers during summer vacations. This is a room of great and unusual proportions, even for a Victorian beach cottage.

The kitchen is reminiscent of old-time country kitchens with its white painted porch liner woodwork, cabinets with glass doors and butcherblock countertops. The collection of cookie jars and schoolhouse lighting fixtures help recall days past.

The master bedroom is a large
rambling room painted a very
pleasing shade of coral pink. Folk
art masks and hooked rugs are
special design elements for this
room.

THIS 3000-SQUARE-FOOT loft is very unique for New York—it has windows on all sides. The clients had very few requests: they wanted two enclosed bedrooms with their own bathrooms, a large living space, housing for their large library, display space for their art collection, and a music area. Also, they requested a quiet, relaxed color palette.

Project Location
New York, New York, USA
Design Firm
Walz Design
Kevin Walz—Principal
Martin Sosa—Project Manager
Photographer
Eduard Heuber

In the design solution, the idea that this is a loft space is always kept in mind—it has that quasi-industrial look, high tech yet romantic. The selection and design of the furnishings add a sophisticated touch to the interior solution. The art plays a large role in the total design. Even though the client wanted a quiet color solution, color and decoration are achieved through sculpture and certain pieces of art furnishings. The high-tech, black steel book racks further add to the overall design theme. The kitchen, with its heavy duty stove pot racks and butcher block finishes, are another important design element here.

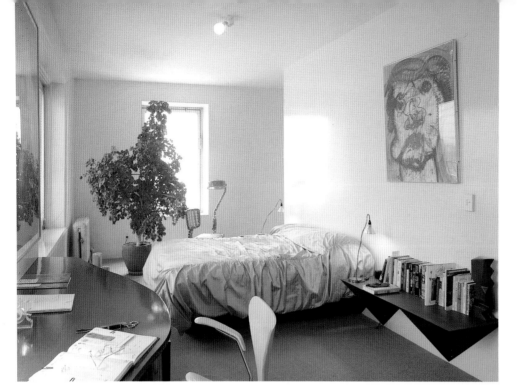

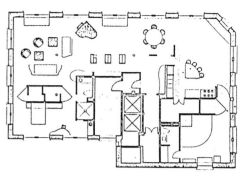

Leonard Colchamiro Architects, PC, AIA
MANHATTAN ATRIUM

THE RENOVATION OF THIS 19th-century townhouse took one year to complete. The architect's assignment was to convert the townhouse from a multiple dwelling, back to its original intended use as a private residence.

Since nearly all of the original detailing was removed during previous conversions, it was decided to use the space dramatically. The client's request for an atrium as the central theme of the design solved this problem beautifully. It allowed for a sense of sweeping proportion and permitted views of multiple levels simultaneously. Additionally, the atrium allowed the owner's extensive art collection to be prominently displayed and seen from a wide variety of different angles.

This concept also helped solve the initial problem of utilizing the space effectively in a deep narrow building. Also, it allowed for light and airflow to be improved. Thus, creating effective circulation.

Project Location
New York, New York, USA
Design Firm
Leonard Colchamiro Architects, PC, AIA
Leonard Colchamiro, Joel Andre—Project Team
Patricia Miller—Interior Designer
Photographer
Ambrose Cucinotta

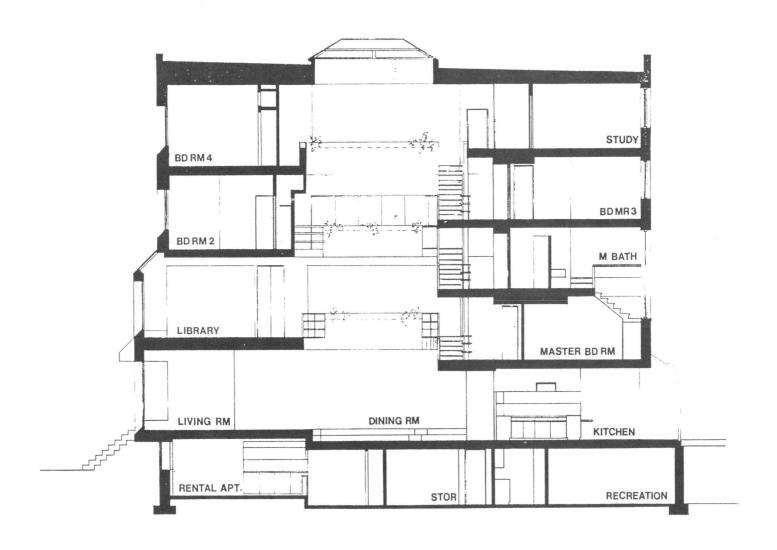

This view of the living room and den from the atrium conveys the commanding expanse of this three-dimensional space. Note the skylight in the den area.

The stair with its tubular steel rails is a major sculptural element in this space.

This space is open and playful with the staircase and the large mural on the wall. The black mirror polished granite floor and tabletop lend a note of sophistication.

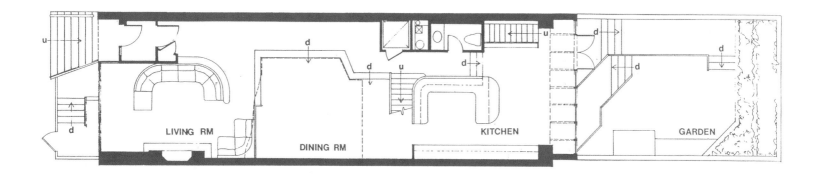

LIVING RM   DINING RM   KITCHEN   GARDEN

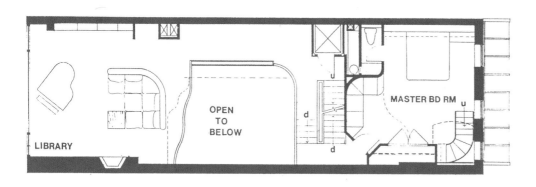

LIBRARY   OPEN TO BELOW   MASTER BD RM

SAUNA   M BATH

The kitchen cabinetry is composed of zebra wood—highly patterned and decorative which adds a touch of warmth and glow to the kitchen space. The polished granite floor continues into the kitchen, thus unifying adjoining areas. The almost lack of color is refreshing and correct; it sharply accents the sculptural aspects of the townhouse.

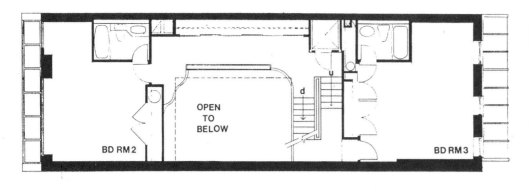

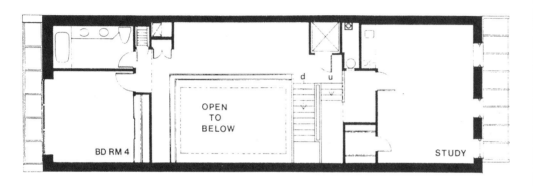

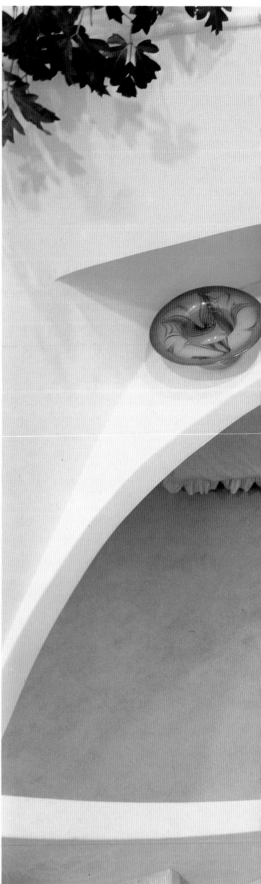

Margaret Helfand Architects
BACHELOR'S APARTMENT

Living Room looking toward Dining Area and Kitchen.

THIS ONE-BEDROOM APARTment overlooks Manhattan's Riverside Drive and the upper west side. The owners' desire to leave the basic floor plan "as is" lead the designers to divide the apartment into quadrants for living: dining, study, kitchen/bath, and the exercise/sleeping/dressing quadrant.

Project Location
New York, New York, USA
Design Firm
Margaret Helfand Architects
Photographer
Paul Warchol

Looking from Kitchen toward end of Video Unit with rotating video monitor.

131

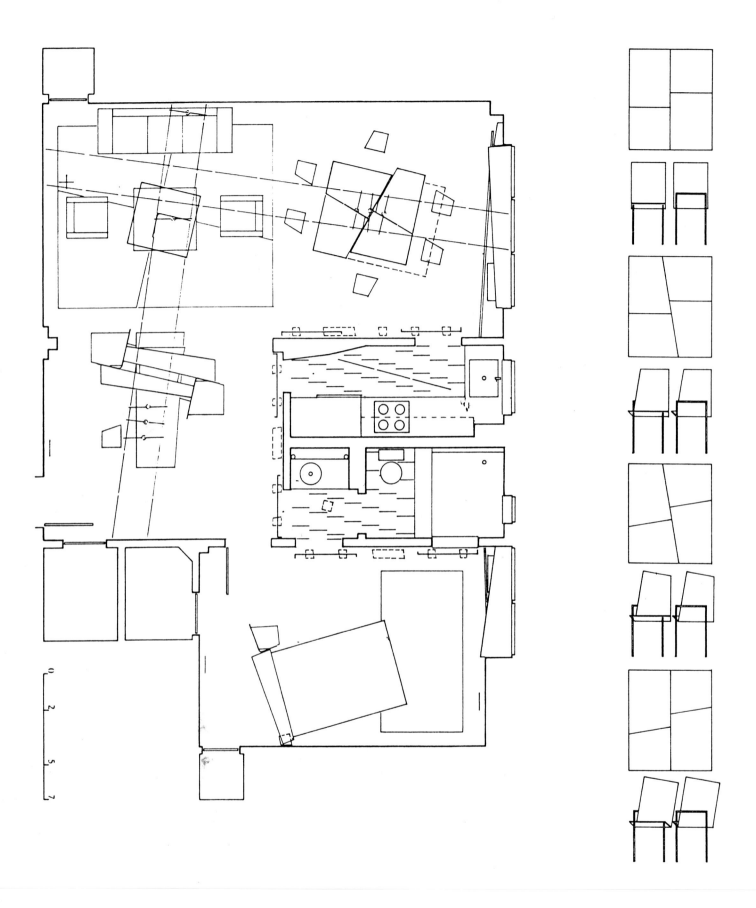

Folded steel plate chairs with rolling dichroic glass screens behind (see chair drawing for concept of chairs)

The kitchen/bath quadrant is the core of the plan. The designers installed sliding doors in the areas with large openings to allow natural light to penetrate their interiors. These openings are covered with rolling translucent panels of three layers of different types of glass; there is a pattern set in the glass panel depicting the floor plan scheme of the adjoining room.

A subtle geometry placement is apparent in these spaces, there are design/sculptural elements of wood, steel, and glass that inter-relate to this geometry. This is an intellectually and thoughtfully designed residence.

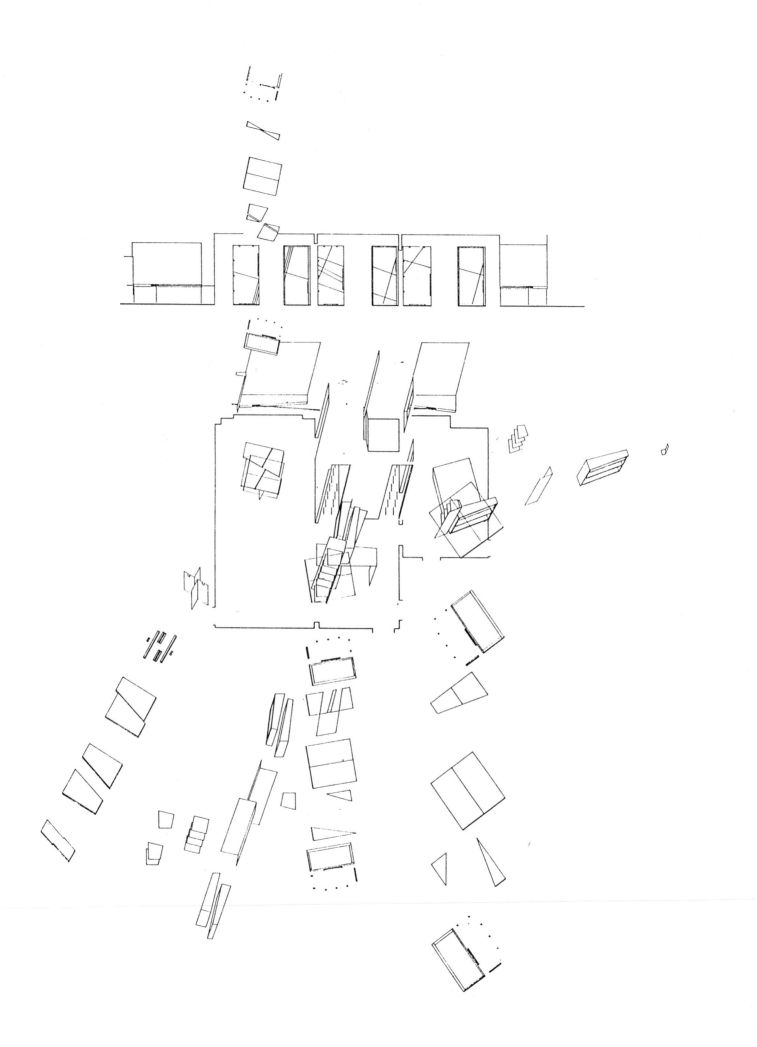

Dining Area including custom extension table and chairs.

Detail of center of steel and cherrywood extension table. (see exploded plan drawing for greater detail)

Looking from Foyer/Study into Dining Area.

Detail of Video Unit and Bookshelves.

Detail of three layer glass screens—handblown irridized glass, dichroic glass and ribbed pressed glass laminated together. (patterns of doors follow floor-plan of adjacent spaces; see exploded plan drawing for greater detail)

Looking from Bedroom through "window" into copper and gray glass mosaic custom bathing pool with rolling dichroic glass screen.

Mariette Himes Gomez
Associates, Inc.
CITY SIMPLICITY

THIS NEW YORK APARTment is comfortable and well thought out. The work is clean and functional, yet, there is a feeling of style and opulence. The eclectic melange of furnishings and accessories recall details from other periods. Colors and materials are laidback and keep the background under control to underscore the main elements of the design idea—traditional with a modern twist.

American folk art is artfully displayed in a delightful way. The spareness of the space reflects the designer's sensitivity of the medium—folk art and architecture work harmoniously in a reflective manner. The overall result is one of varying texture, pattern and shape that contrasts, yet compliments, one another.

This over view of the living room gives one a quick idea of the diverse taste and interest of the client—American Folk Art and Classic American Furniture. The background of this apartment is quiet and sets-up a simple backdrop for a dialog between art and furniture.

This majestic entry space is purposefully left bare and minimal—the art and the furniture create the statement. The collection of furnishings includes a number of Shaker pieces as well as beautiful 18th and 19th century pieces.

Project Location
New York, New York, USA
Design Firm
Mariette Himes Gomez Associates, Inc.
Mariette Himes Gomez—President
Photographer
Billy Cunningham

This dining room has an interesting collection of painted and non-painted Windsor chairs around an 18th century farm table. Folk art and other painted pieces complete this ensemble.

The kitchen is contemporary in design and lay-out but has decorative ideas and spirit in other time periods. The hood over the center island recalls the early 20th century when this apartment building was erected. The wide plank wood floors are the same one would expect in a Vermont farmhouse in the early 19th century.

Mel Dwork Inc.

DESIGNER'S ABODE

Project Location
New York, New York, USA
Design Firm
Melvin Dwork, Inc.
Interior Designer
Melvin Dwork
Photographer
John Hall

THIS APARTMENT'S DESIGN is geared toward showcasing the client's beautiful art collection. Neutral colors and earthtones predominate, so as not to detract from the art. Most of the walls throughout the house are painted off-white with many of the architectural elements (i.e. support columns) painted black green. The study's walls are painted black green to contrast with the predominance of black and white art.

Primitive art, live plantings, tongue and groove pine flooring and black leather furniture designed by Melvin Dwork create a harmonious eclectic look.

The bedroom hall contains a pleasing melange of furnishings and art: an 18th century slipper chair in mahogany signed Jacob, an 18th century lacquer leather trunk, a pair of wood African antelope heads, a small black-and-white drawing by Bernard Venet, and a Navajo blanket viewed in the mirror.

A view of the enclosed desk area. An 18th century blanc de chine vase was converted into a table lamp.

In the study, a dramatic table-
scape is created via miscellaneous
primitive African and Australian art.

In the living area, looking toward the entrance and kitchen is an early American painted wood chair. The slipper chair was designed by Melvin Dwork. A Korean chimney pot sits on the counter, a baboon head sits on a miniature African stool.

Entry door area with kitchen on left. A planter's palm defines the entrance.

Michael de Santis

A Place to Bike and Hike

Project Location
Big Canoe, Georgia, USA
Design Firm
Michael de Santis
Photographer
Bart Wrisley

The exterior of the house is deceivingly small, especially with the use of a porte cochere.

THIS HOUSE IS DECEIVING from the exterior, especially with the porte cochere. The interior space soars with its pitched ceiling and large window expanses. The exterior deck brings the outside indoors. The interior furnishings nicely reflect this "natural leaning." The master bed is constructed of bleached logs, doweled together. A secondary design/decorative motif, the American Indian and the Southwest, predominates. The Southwest idea is also pervasive and evident in the dining area and guest bedrooms. Don't forget the cowboy boots that seem to allude to the inhabitants of this fantastic house.

The exterior deck of the home invites the outdoors inside.

The large, natural stone fireplace dominates the living room.

The interior soars with its pitched ceiling and large expanse of windows.

Furnishings and art reflect on designs that predominate in the Southwest. Note native American art adds dramatic color and punch to the rooms.

The timber type bed is appropriate for this design. The bed cover recalls Navajo-type blanket designs.

The guest bedroom has an American Indian inspired bed and on the wall above the headboard there is a native tribal coat. The walls are knotty pine.

Michael LaRocca Interiors
ELEGANT ESCAPE

This living room recalls the best of the design ideas for American country homes of the early 20th Century. Michael LaRocca has updated that concept and yet retained all the best of the past and integrated it with the spirit of today.

THIS HOUSE BUILT IN THE late '20s is modeled after British manor houses. This delightful house has a restrained exuberance, yet, there are still little fun quirks to be found and cherished. The living room focuses on the magnificent marble fireplace mantle and the terra cotta frame around the firebox. The wall color harkens back to rich 18th century tones, noted for their glow and luminosity. The dining room, with its dark green walls, sets another tone and mood for the house. The natural daylight flooding in through oversize windows helps to enliven these interior spaces.

Project Location
Greenwich, Connecticut, USA
Design Firm
Michael LaRocca Interiors
Photographers
Antoine Bootz and Darwin Davidson (p. 156)

This living room has beautiful coloring, wonderful natural light and
the furnishings and art works
unify to create a masterful blend
of many ideas and time periods.

The furnishings are scaled to the room and are very comfortable yet elegant. The red Louis XV fireplace creates the focus for this space.

The windows are large and expansive and bring the out-of-doors inside.

The kitchen was designed to accommodate husband and wife cooking together; there is a large center island which houses commercial cooking equipment. The island countertop is polished granite, and the same material is found in four inch squares off-set in the floor which is 12" hand-made terra cotta tile from Provence.

All the cabinetry in the kitchen is American Cherry in its natural color. All countertops other than the center island are of 3" thick custom cherry butcherblock.

The dining room is a very cozy
and comfortable room. The walls
are dark green and the furnishings are antique. All the molding
and woodwork are original to the
home.

Nick Calder Designs

FUN & FANTASY

There is a lot happening in this room—from the faux finish pony skins to the other beautifully finished walls. The furnishings are eclectic and highly unusual.

THIS UNIQUE DESIGN EXpression is fun and serious at the same moment. The black-and-white pony skin motif is wittily carried throughout the space and is found in the most unexpected places. It keeps good company with the furnishings—19th century antiques and 20th century Art Deco pieces.

The classic black-and-white decorative idea contrasts nicely with the warm, sienna-toned wall. The bedroom further carries out this classic motif with the small spotted chair and a sprinkling of Dalmatian spots.

Color, pattern, texture and shape are the main elements utilized throughout this entire residence. The design is unrestrained and exuberant, and this philosophy is what makes this design concept so successful.

Project Location
New York, New York, USA
Design Firm
Nick Calder Designs
Photographer
Julio Pedro (Deceased)
Faux Painting–Walls
Chuck Hittinger

This dining alcove has a graphic presentation also—there is the bold black and white stripe on the wrought iron chairs and you have the pony skin next to a painted textured finish, all framed out with picture moldings into panels.

This is a very graphic concept—using pony skin as a design motif. This is lighthearted fantasy, and serious, all at the same time.

Noel Jeffrey Inc.

DECO DELIGHT

THIS LUXURIOUS NEW YORK City apartment recalls its Art Deco heritage; Noel Jeffrey freely interprets the period with additions of more up-to-date furnishings that relate to this heritage. The flooring is lightened oak that has an endless feel. The light, softly-colored, pastel wall adds to this sense of spaciousness. The seat-ing in the living room is soft and voluptuous. Black lacquer used in the furnishings recalls the Art Deco period. The fireplace surround and the background wall are reminiscent of Normandie. The lighting through-out the apartment is well designed—casting shadows where needed and adding sparkle to important spots.

Project Location
New York, New York, USA
Design Firm
Noel Jeffrey Inc.
Noel Jeffrey—Designer
Photographer
Kari Havisto

This apartment exudes Art Deco, especially apparent when viewing the fireplace surround. The woodwork wall that surrounds this Art Deco masterpiece reinforces this spirit.

This is a small sitting room overlooking the terrace. The floor is richly covered in marble and the furnishings recall the Art Deco period.

The master bedroom has a raised sitting area in a glasshouse structure. The room is painted a soft pink color and all the other finishes reflect this color concept.

This intimate semi-circular greenhouse space is a great place to snuggle-up while reading a book; it overlooks a dining terrace with lots of planting and sculpture.

In the bedroom, the beige on beige tonal aspect is indeed soothing; it is a quiet haven away from the frenetic city below.

Manhattan Opulence

Color is important to this design and you see many variations of red and pink in this small sitting room. The style here is opulent and rich.

THE COLOR INSPIRATION for this apartment must have been a Tuscan Villa; the lush ambience of these rooms with their splendid detailing evokes this feeling. The great room boasts a polished stone floor with a grand portal. The doors/gates would seem at home in an Italian Villa; the wall hung tapestry suggests architectural fantasy and foliage with romping nymphs. The three-dimensional frieze around the perimeter of the room adds a great deal of interest and charm.

Project Location
New York, New York, USA
Design Firm
Noel Jeffrey, Inc.
Noel Jeffrey – Designer
Photographer
Peter Vitale

The sitting area off the dining room is dominated by a large painted allegorical paneled screen. The coloring evokes a sense of Italy, but the subject matter suggests early Hellenic Greece. In addition, this sitting area contains well-known French Art Deco posters. Another part of this area contains a sofa in a soft sea green, more late 19th century art work and French Directoire accessories.

The frontal view of the painted, paneled screen shows its strong decorative effect; the painting style recalls the Art Deco painting at Rockefeller Center in New York. The French Desk with ivory inlay is by cabinetmaker Jean Dunnand.

This room opens onto a dining room containing colorful '20s and '30s French posters. The chair and draped table harken to the Directoire period.

The walls are a variation of Tuscan Red and the art works and accessories are varied and interesting. The dark green upholstered seating elements offer a nice contrast to the wall color.

Art Deco is recalled in this room through the posters and the two lounge chairs.

This small dining room utilizes a simple, straightforward design idea—let the art work become the focus. The entrance doors recall classical Roman architectural motifs.

This too is a classical space—Roman in feeling and detail. The marble floor adds a flourish of elegance to this space.

This small study area is divided from the dining room by a decorative screen with classical allusions and details. In this area we see a beautiful Art Deco desk by Ruhlman.

The master bedroom repeats the color scheme of the apartment; The walls are covered with damask. Note the unusual molding at the ceiling.

The master bathroom continues the European elegance of the rest of the apartment. The black marble walls create a dramatic background.

ROOMS WITH A VIEW

This apartment on Fifth Avenue in New York City looks out onto Central Park and the West Side. The views are magical and the windows let a great deal of natural light into the interior spaces.

THIS IS AN APARTMENT OF high style and great art! The richness of this combination is inspirational. The elevator entryway gives an instant first impression that this place is special—rich wood paneling, stone flooring, and abundant art. The barrel-vaulted space is charming and architecturally unusual for such a small space. The Versailles parquet in the main public areas creates a soft neutral background for the furnishings, plants, and art. The paintings seem to float away from the walls. The red velour seating, along with the rich dark wood paneling, give this room a rich, dark headiness that is lightened by the Picasso portrait on the wall and the small Henry Moore Macquette on the oval marble table.

The corridor is replete with art— the Louise Nevelsons work well with the Juan Miro. The mirror wall doubles their visual impact.

The master bedroom is also filled with art. This rich room is colored with pink-hued walls, contains burl cabinetry and has a lush upholstered window seating area. The cabinetry ledge along the far wall is a great space to display changing art work.

Project Location
New York, New York, USA
Design Firm
Noel Jeffrey Inc.
Noel Jeffrey – Designer
Photographer
Jaime Ardiles-Arce

The Miro painting sets the design
idea for this room; these are
graphic and dramatic works of art
and the furnishings are down-
played. The walls are a soft pink
color and the wood parquet floor
picks up this pink tone.

Another passageway is filled with plants, erupting out of illuminated niches. The mirror cabinetry surfaces add to the mystery and illusion.

The dining room is dominated by a large Botero painting and a splendid rosewood dining table. The table is set with whimsical metallic birds which in turn hold floating blossoms. The entrance to this room is flanked by a male and female bronze figure also by Botero.

The passageway becomes an art
gallery; the left wall is a bronze
tint mirror panel reflecting the
Nevelson sculpture and the other
works of art.

The dining room features painting and sculpture by Botero. The table is set with interesting peacock dishes holding floating blossoms.

The view in the evening is spectacular — the towers of Manhattan come alive as the evening grows old.

The master bedroom has its own special art works too. Moire covered walls add a cozy feeling to the space, and the window seat offers that great city view.

The sitting room just off the dining room is richly covered in rosewood paneling and the seating units are upholstered in velour. The Picasso painting establishes the color palette.

The master bath looks out onto
Manhattan also. The countertop
was kept low so that the view
would not be obstructed yet the
custom stainless steel sink is at
the correct height.

HIGH RISE APARTMENT

This view of the living room illustrates the raised platform that separates the music end of the living room from the conversation end of the room. The piano poster on the wall is graphic and striking.

T HIS MASTER BEDROOM suite is at once sculptural, architectural and charmingly alluring. The raised platform with its sensuous built-in seating/ reading area is inviting. The master bed faces the media wall and a small personal library. A work area is located to the side. The blue/gray/ beige color scheme is quite different and understated.

Project Location
New York, New York, USA
Design Firm
Noel Jeffrey Inc.
Photographer
Peter Aaron

This is the built-in seating on a raised platform in the master suite. Bookshelves and framed artworks enclose the windows.

The dining room continues the art idea—framed French posters from the 1920s and 30s. The sections of mirror behind the serving shelf reflect the view beyond.

The typical New York high rise bathroom (narrow, but with a view) has been expanded with glass, mirrors, and a beige tone grided tile used on all surfaces. Polished steel/chrome hardware is a refreshing change from more conventional master baths.

The kitchen is also typical for high rises—long and narrow, with high ceilings. The solution was an adaptive reuse of existing early 20th century upper cabinetry, married to late 20th century plastic laminate cabinetry with oak hardware/trim. The large expansive windows give the room a more spacious feel—light and airy. The track lighting with barn doors on the fixtures brings in a "high-tech" attitude.

The raised platform living room has a strong focal point—the sculptural black lacquered grand piano, which in turn is reinforced by a

magnificent Art Deco poster featuring the "Piano." This room also focuses on a built-in television monitor that rises up from the coffee table—a project screen secretly lowers from a recess in the ceiling at the opposite end of the room. The beige/shell pink color scheme is quiet and relaxing.

The Dining room color scheme is continued from the living room. The mirror-paneled wall reflects the opposite window wall and opens up the room. The wood dining table adds warmth to the space; the French Art Nouveau poster contributes to this mood.

This is a simple, well-organized kitchen. The upper cabinetry reflects what one would find in a 1920s New York City apartment, while the lower cabinets are more contemporary. There is a dining alcove at the end of the kitchen.

This is a bedroom for a little girl—
it's charming and unique. The antique bed and the raised
platform at the window area add
to the room s charm.

The guest bathroom is simple—
tile floor and walls. There is a window in the shower.

The master bedroom has a raised
platform; the bed faces a media
wall and there is a comfortable
built-in seating unit to the right.

Ojinaga

BARCELONA PENTHOUSE

The soaring height of the ceiling allowed for a hillock to be installed to create a duplex.

Project Location
Barcelona, Spain
Design Firm
Ojinaga, S.C.P. Interior and Architecture Studio
Interior Designers
Carlos Ojinaga Erill
Josefina Gomez Martin
Architect
Carlos Ojinaga Gill
Photographer
J. Mundo

THE CLIENT FOR THIS apartment, a single executive for a major financial company in Barcelona, wanted a space that would accommodate his lifestyle.

Ojinaga successfully created a duplex penthouse for their client. Their objective was to create an interior designed space that culled elements from neoclassical and modern styles. The firm designed the exterior and interior spaces, as well as most of the furniture; this was done to create a unified space that worked harmoniously with all elements.

The color scheme for this apartment is a neutral palette. Furniture shapes are reminiscent of the neoclassical sytle.

Uplights positioned at the tops of columns provide pleasing ambient light that highlights architectural detailings.

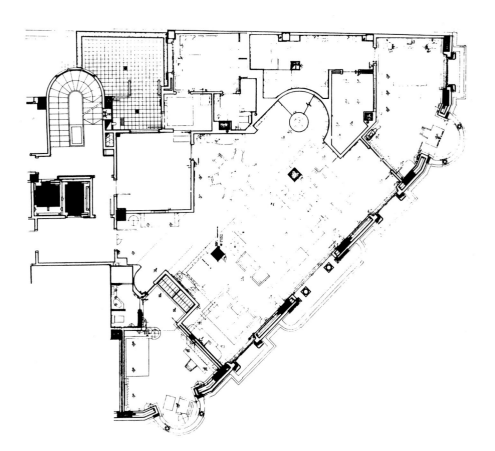

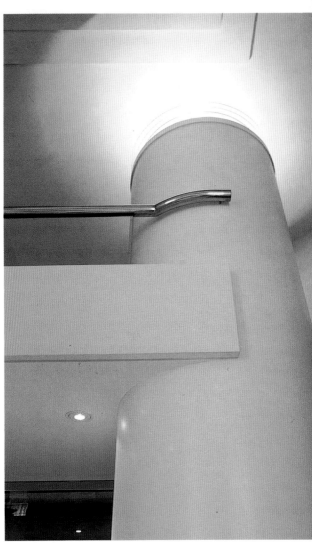

The architectural concept for this
apartment is monolithic and dramatic. These spaces are large and
ceiling heights are quite generous. This main seating area
backs-up to and is overlooked by
a mezzanine with a regulation-
sized pool table.

The architecture has a fluid feeling and seems to flow nicely. The white color of these spaces further add to this sense. This dining area is adjacent to the living space and is under the mezzanine.

This is the mezzanine overlooking the living/dining space.

The apartment was completely void of any architectural elements. A huge distance between the floor and ceiling allowed the designers to introduce a hillock, thus transforming the apartment into a bi-level duplex. The main obstacle was to create the necessary architectural structures to sustain the hillock, without detracting from the space. A longitudinal beam (similar to a railing) was utilized to support the hillock. The result is breathtaking.

Black marble accents provide a dramatic counterpoint in the bathroom.

A grey granite floor with matching backsplash and countertop provide rich touches in the kitchen.

The design of this vanity in the master bathroom becomes even more dramatic when the background is clear mirror panels. Lighting is from wall sconces right and left of the vanity.

Ronn Jaffe Associates

Barbara Bush Grand Salon

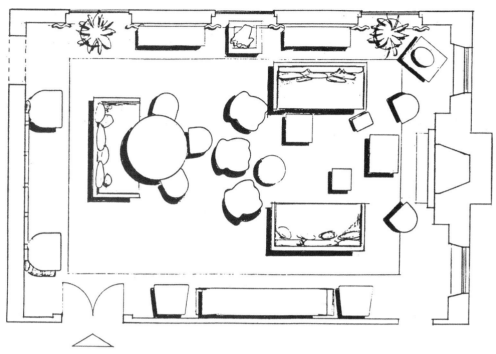

In plan you can readily see how large this grand room really is. The room suggests a number of conversation areas and several focal points. This is a very eclectic melange of concepts, decoration, art and ideas.

THIS 750-SQUARE FOOT space is a large and graciously proportioned room—the space reinforces its grand concept. This is a room for entertaining in a grand manner. This is a very important room and the furnishings and art seem to underlie this concept. The room has beautiful antiques and art work of the first order. The space is laid-out with cluster seating, with small areas of conversational grouping. This room is a reminder of 19th century design ideas—the paintings begin to fill the walls in groupings, with a profusion of sculptural art. The materials and finishes are rich and opulent. The coral lacquered ceiling is a strong horizontal statement and adds needed psychological height. The blue silk covered sofas further underscore the richness of the concept.

Project Location
Washington, District of Columbia, USA
Design Firm
Ronn Jaffe Associates
Ronn Jaffe—President
Mars Jaffe—Vice President
Photographer
Gordon Beall

LEMPICKA LIBRARY

Project Location
Avenel-Potomac, Maryland, USA
Design Firm
Ronn Jaffe Associates
Ronn Jaffe—President
Mars Jaffe—Vice President
Photographer
Mark Borchelt

THIS 450-SQUARE-FOOT space was originally designed in the fifties; Ronn Jaffe brought this space back to life in an inventive and monumental way. The elliptical shape of the room was reinforced through a new architectural approach—the introduction of columns, additional woodworking/cabinetry and bulky furnishings in better scale with the space. The new feeling is a backward nod to Biedermeier Design,

The sweeping generous curves add much interest to this beautifully executed space. The lighting in the cove ceiling adds another dimension to this room. The polished black granite floor gives a rich, finished feeling.

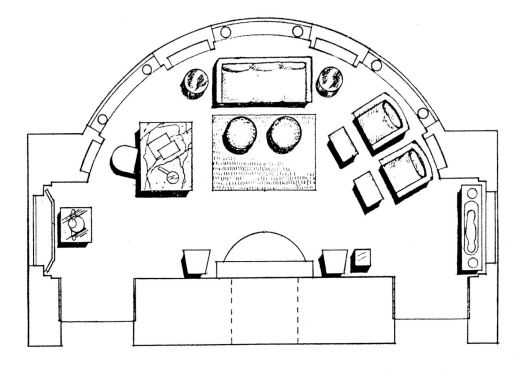

with its contrasting wood work and decoratively restrained stenciled work. The black granite floor and fireplace surround add an unmistakable elegance to the space; the area carpets and furnishings seem to float in the space. The cove ceiling with its indirect lighting further adds to the charm and ambience of the total space. The lighting is directed toward the bookcases, emphasizing the architectural statement.

The massive stone fireplace surround completes the elevations of the Lempicka Library. The richness of the wall paneling with its black squares at the crown molding line contrasts with the stone of the surround.

Sandra Nunnerley Designs
TALL WINDOWS TOWNHOUSE

THIS CHARMING, QUIET IN-terior belies its location in New York City.

The parlor level has a generous ceiling height and contains a plethora of architectural detailing—from the stair banister, to the ornate moldings, to the detailed baseboard.

The fireplace harkens to sim-plified 19th-century design. The art deco chairs, around the hearth, pro-vide a nice counterpoint to the almost severe lines of the surround.

This room reflects all the natural light coming in through the majestic casements. The pink tone of the wall color is fur-ther enhanced by the color, pattern and texture of the fur-nishings.

Tall windows allow an abundance of natural light to filter into inte-rior spaces.

Project Location
New York, New York, USA
Design Firm
Sandra Nunnerley Designs
Photographer
Jon Jensen
All photographs reprinted with permission © 1990
Metropolitan Home.

Another seating area, located within the parlor, is anchored by a sofa. The overall color scheme is serene, soft and rich imparting a warm feel. The room is enhanced by an abundance of natural light filtering in through the tall windows.

This room has a very serene feeling overall—the color palette, natural light, and furnishings all contribute to this ambience.

Geometric fabric on many of the upholstered pieces emphasizes the architecture.

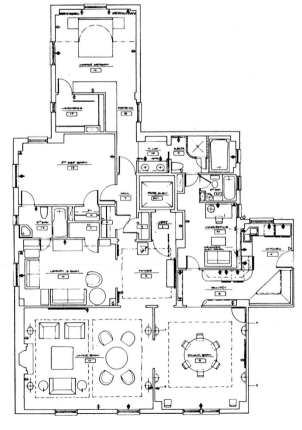

URBAN TRANQUILITY

The furnishings are done predominantly in white and cream, imparting a serene, opulent air.

Project Location
New York, New York, USA
Design Firm
Sandra Nunnerley Designs
Photographer
John Hall

THIS OPULENT NEW YORK
City apartment expresses a
sense of place that is
unique; the purity and
whiteness of the elements that constitute the design are unusual, clean
and spare. Yet, small details and accessories give the space character
and panache. The materials utilized,
including the upholstery and various
wood finishes, add to this impression
of "spare elegance." The furnishings
are minimal and work with this overall "restrained" philosophy to
effectively portray the feeling of opulence and comfort.

This dining area is a part of the main living space—the furniture and furnishings are all in similar color families and the textures all relate to one another. The whole apartment has an air of casual chaos.

The bedroom is dominated by a
large 19th century cabinet. The
walls relate to the rest of the
apartment, as do all the other
furnishings.

There is a wonderful sense of a build-up of layers on top of layers—many soft related colors and fabrics create a richness and a soft natural beauty.

Scott Bromley Interiors

ARCHITECTURAL STATEMENT

This is drama—architectural drama, a Karnack Temple approach in miniature. The vista at the end is contemporary and sculptural.

THIS NEW YORK APARTment interior places special emphasis on the architecture of the space, namely, the columns with their intricate detailing.

The entrance hallway, with its Karnack-like columnar arrangement is stately and dramatic. The sculpture at the end of the hallway/gallery is appropriate and provides an interesting finish point to this vista.

The focal point of the living space is the angled fireplace. The brass molding is a subtle, yet rich detail along the perimeter of the ceiling.

The dining space opens off the hallway and contains a two-table seating arrangement, which nicely breaks up the area. The highly-reflective tabletops add an interesting layer of depth. The lighting and colors used throughout the space adds punch to the architecture and highlights important details.

The master bedroom suite is a cool contrast to the rest of the apartment. The serene mauve color scheme, with its rich fabrics, provides a nice foil.

Project Location
New York, New York, USA
Design Firm
Bromley Caldari Architects PC
Photographer
Jaime Ardiles-Arce

The artwork and brass accents imbue an oriental flavor to the overall design. In the master bath, the mauve color scheme is subtly alluded to by the mauve/lilac neon lighting in the alcove above the vanity.

The kitchen continues the restrained colors found throughout the rest of the public spaces. Bleached wood floors and stone on the work surfaces provide a natural brightness and texture to the area. The beautifully-constructed cabinetry with its impressive detailing juxtaposes nicely with the other elements that comprise this kitchen. Even the pot rack, located above the central work island, transforms into a piece of artwork when left bare.

The architectural sculpture of the over fireplace sets-up the focal point of the living space. All the seating units are grouped around the fireplace. The lighting is well designed—from recessed cove lighting to uplighting and floor lamps.

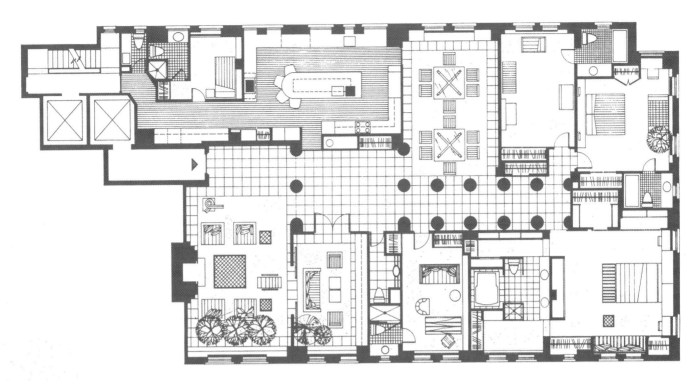

The dining room doesn't lack from its own dramatics—the columnar motif becomes one wall of this dining room and the lighting solution is quite spectacular.

The kitchen has a free-standing
work island that also doubles as a
dining spot. The sculptural rack
over this island is designed to
hold pots and pans.

The den is very dark, comtempla-
tive, and serious in mood. The
antique desk is French.

The master bedroom is soft in color—mauves, purples, and pinks. The lighting is dramatic. All the furnishings are upholstered.

The master bathroom has a polished black granite countertop, walls and floor of pink marble and a custom shower enclosure fitted in brass.

SHOWCASING ART

THIS SPACIOUS APARTMENT is quite large with a lot of open space. The architect has used an architectural vocabulary to set the design mood, carried through in every detail, color, finish and lighting design. The elements and space flow together to create a unified whole.

Of special interest is the ceiling treatment—coves with recessed lighting in some areas, while other ceiling areas contain exposed neon tubing that connects adjoining spaces.

One of Scott Bromley's signature design elements is contained here, the angled and pitched column detail.

In the kitchen, the open airy feeling is expressed with restrained details, like the plainly detailed cabinetry.

The background in this apartment is fairly neutral and lets the architecture and the art make the design statement. Here, a black lacquered baby grand piano becomes a piece of free-standing sculpture next to a Miro painting.

Project Location
New York, New York, USA
Design Firm
Bromley Caldari Architects PC
Photographer
Jaime Ardiles-Arce

This view of the living room reveals the columnar architectural
concept of these spaces. Cove
lighting gives the ceiling that ex-
tra-added dimension.

A dramatic note in this space is the angled, gridded glass wall highlighted with blue neon. This architectural element almost serves as a piece of art. The grid idea is repeated throughout the apartment, even in the master bath. A glass wall is located near the tub area. The marble surfacing used on the walls, floor and vanity are all the same type. Yet, this design element along with the mirrors adds volume to this space.

The dining room has the same color palette as the other public spaces.

215

The media room fits into the rest of the concept—the color, the lighting, and the architecture.

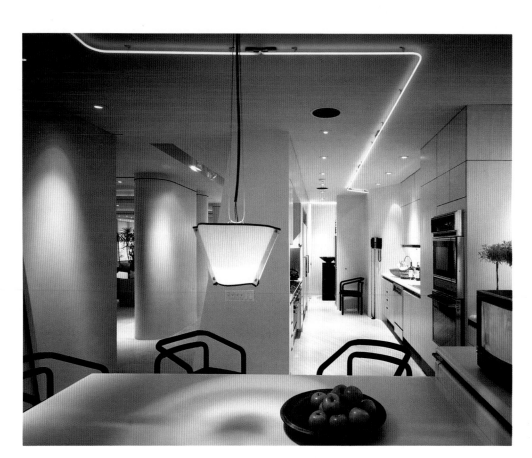

The kitchen also fits into the rest of these public spaces conceptually. Here, neon cove tube lighting is exposed and becomes a design feature mounted onto the ceiling.

This is the master bathroom. The angled diffused glass grid wall emits light from the main public spaces. The black and white polished marble is used lavishly on floor, walls and vanity top.

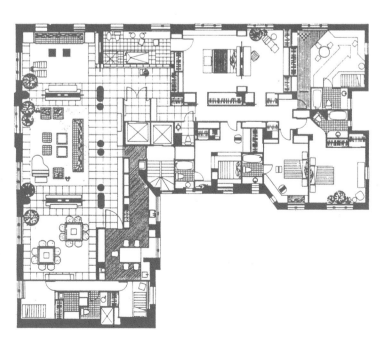

HIGH-TECH LUXURY

The angled walls are the dramatic
statement here. The cove lighting
works well and the views from
the apartment windows are
terrific.

THE ANGLED WALLS IN THIS
apartment serve as the main
architectural statement in
this interior design. This
high-tech oriented space contains a
myriad of wizardry, from its control
panels to its special lighting effects.

The ceiling channel highlighted
with pink neon pulls you into the
space. The angled wall in the living

Project Location
New York, New York, USA
Design Firm
Bromley Caldari Architects PC
Photographer
Jaime Ardiles-Arce

room divides the media center from the dining room. This same wall also provides a dramatic niche in the dining room to display a collection of Picasso ceramics. The chandelier over the dining table provides task lighting, and the angled wall also contains a recessed cove that houses an array of special lighting devices.

Highly-polished black granite is used as a border in the floor of the public spaces and delineates each area.

This is the bar—at a very appropriate place within the apartment—at the entrance! The lighting in the ceiling adds a bit of whimsy to the space.

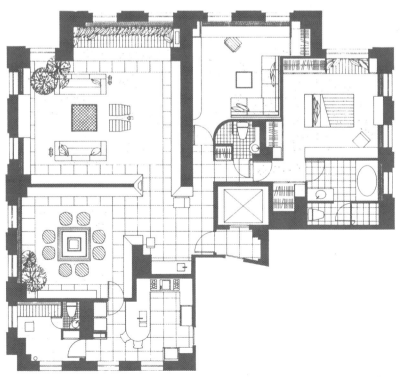

The pink recessed angular lighting cove pulls you into the dining room with its dramatic illuminated display coved walls. The lighting device/sculpture over the frosted and clear glass dining table is a conversation stopper.

The kitchen adjoins the dining area. A salt-and-pepper granite countertop lends a note of elegance to this simple, unencumbered design.

The master bedroom and sitting room are well-designed and highly understated. The colors are soft and restful and do not detract from the exceptional view.

Thomas Hauser Design Ltd.
ATELIER/RESIDENCE & OFFICE

This dual purpose space is a unique and interesting solution. There are great ideas of space planning along with sculptural concepts.

Project Location
New York, New York, USA
Design Firm
Thomas Hauser Design Ltd.
Thomas Hauser—President
Henry Miller—Design Assistant
Photographer
Peter Paige

THE INTENTION OF THE designer was to transform a raw loft space of approximately 1000 square feet into a combined residence and office. The primary goal was the most efficient use of the existing space. At the commencement of the project the space was one level and without interior walls. It had poured concrete floors, exposed concrete support beams and three structural columns.

Unusual features included: 12'3" ceilings and large sliding glass windows with transoms that afford southern exposure.

The designer's first step was to sheet-rock all existing structural beams and the perimeter wall. Our intention was to refine and enhance the sculptural qualities of the supporting beams, establishing a rhythmic progression of form which would set the tone for the rest of the design concept.

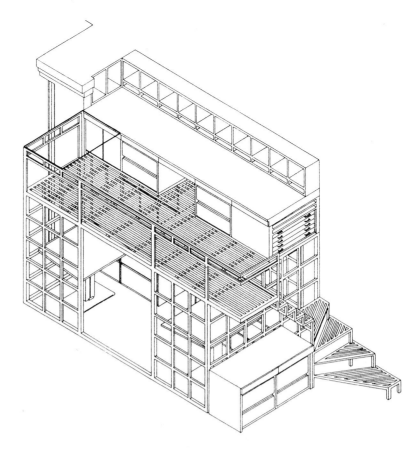

This view is rich in color and texture—the stair becomes a sculptural object in this very simple, serene space. This is the approach to the sleeping quarters.

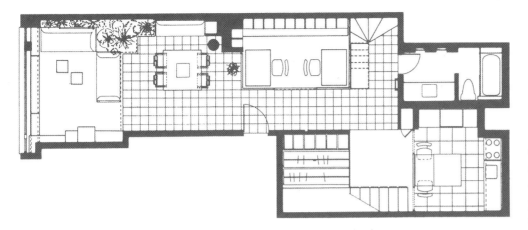

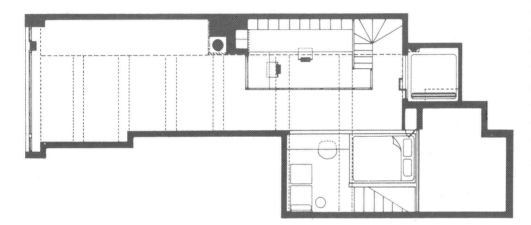

Because of the multi-function purposes intended for the space as both office and residence, we took advantage of the unusually high ceilings to establish second levels in three places.

The first is the bedroom, lounge and dressing area. By raising a second floor 54' above the original, they were able to supply a comfortable lounge area with a ceiling height of 7'. This area is reached by open stairs running along the perimeter wall. By raising the cantilevered bed platform an additional 30", we increased the clearance on level I under the platform to 81". This became the dressing area. To increase the functionality of this area, we provided pull-out trolleys faced with mirrors, and drawer space concealed in the stairway.

This is a view to the living quarters on the loft level. Below is the office quarters.

This is a view of the office quarters. The steel structure is two levels and houses two work stations on each level.

The second use of two levels is in the guest loft which is carved into the unused space above the bathroom.

The third use of two levels is the fabrication of an open steel structure which is attached to the wall opposite the bedroom, and incorporates the grid and square motif which is repeated throughout the design. On the first level this structure houses: two drafting stations, a clerical/administrative area, design resource library, general filing space and storage. On the second level are the owner's private office, personal library, and storage for architectural drawings and project notes. The bold lines of the steel create a screen or lattice-like effect, and set the tone for the rest of the space.

In the balance of the space, which is allocated to kitchen, dining/conference area and living room, the original 12′3″ ceilings remain. The living room is separated from the dining/conference area both by the use of contrasting texture (marble against carpet) and by the construction of a low platform to create a step up. Storage in the kitchen is constructed entirely of industrial filing cabinets. The geometric motifs recur throughout as both void and solid forms.

Wolk Design

FLORIDA FANTASY

This is an elaborate fantasy house—the plan is expressive and interesting. The interiors are open, colorful, and fun.

Project Location
Miami, Florida, USA
Design Firm
Michael Wolk Design
Michael Wolk—Principal
Photographer
Dan Forer, Forer Inc.

THIS APPROXIMATELY 6500-square-foot, two-story residence was originally built in 1947, with an addition installed in the 1960s. The challenge was to renovate the existing house with minor structural changes to accommodate a family of six, not including two live-in housekeepers.

All bathrooms, kitchen and family room were completely gutted and refitted with new cabinetry, floors, and electrical work.

Some of the furniture in the house was designed by Michael Wolk including: the custom lounge chair and coffee table (living room), the dining room table, and the custom media unit and coffee table (family room).

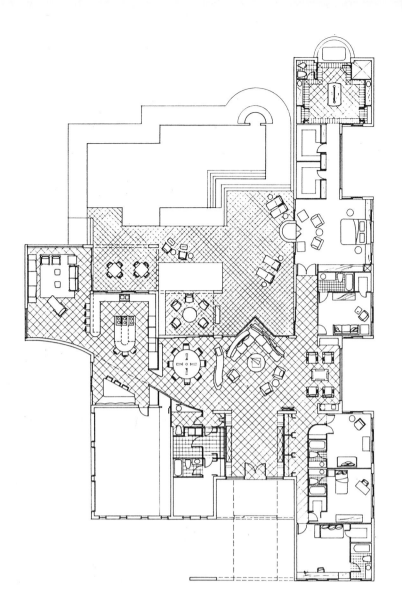

The entrance to this house is light and airy, thanks to the oculus of a skylight. The square of polished marble sets-off this space in a tranquil, creative manner.

This photograph illustrates how interior walls can be molded and opened-up to reveal interesting forms, light and shadow.

The furnishings here are custom-designed for the space and they all relate nicely. The built-in cabinetry fits into the scheme of things, and the white walls reflect lots of natural Florida light.

This master bedroom has well-designed, built-in cabinetry, in several types of wood. The bed headboard is a piece of sculpture in itself and has a warmth and richness that is unexpected in most modern interiors.

The master bathroom is all sparkle and glow through the curving glass block wall. The bathtub is given a ceremonial position on the elevated marble covered platform with a backdrop of glass block—not unlike being on stage.

Living with Architecture and Art

This sophisticated living space is open and comfortable; the island of carpet anchors down this grouping. The fabrics and colors in the furniture are monochromatic, yet there is lots of color and pattern throughout the house. The artwork contributes greatly to this design approach.

THIS APPROXIMATE 8000-square-foot residence, originally a spec home, was redesigned to accommodate the needs of the occupants—a couple with two children, one on the way, and a live-in housekeeper.

The symmetrical to random floor pattern, consisting of unfilled honed travertine, with polished filled marble accents, reflects the activities and seating areas of the house. The entry pattern is symmetrical to enhance the formality of the entrance. As you move into the living area, the pattern is more freely placed to compliment the spacious movement of the furniture layout.

By removing a freestanding fireplace that originally divided the living and dining areas, the impact of one great room was achieved. A 14-foot bar was also removed to allow for an additional seating area off the living room.

Adjacent to this seating area, a curved glass block was changed to fluted glass to achieve consistency with the fluted glass entry panels flanking the front door.

The designer was responsible for all custom built-ins and furniture throughout the residence.

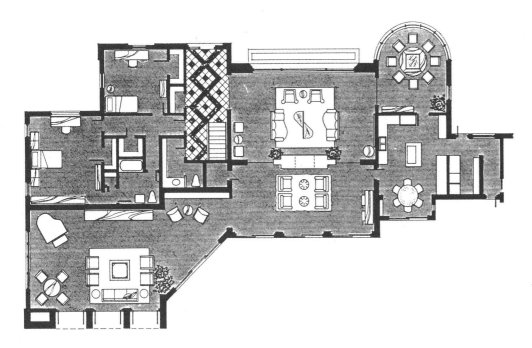

Project Location
Miami, Florida, USA
Design Firm
Michael Wolk Design
Michael Wolk—Principal
Photographer
Dan Forer, Forer Inc.

The artwork gives a great deal of punch to these spaces — they add warmth, color, and a lively spirit.

The vertical tongue-and-groove wood panels painted white add a textural note.

This entrance hall is a powerful space with its two-tone bold, marble graphic floor. The black lacquer pedestals work well in this warm rich space, and the wall color reflects the terra cotta of the marble squares. The white enamel trim color on the doors and base makes the total effect appear even more crisp and clean.

APPENDIX

A and D Wejchert, Architects
23 Lower Baggot Street
Dublin 2
Ireland

Anderson/Schwartz, Architects
40 Hudson Street
New York, NY 10013

Barbara and Michael Orenstein
40 East 88th Street
New York, NY 10128

Bruce Bierman Design, Inc.
29 West 15th Street
New York, NY 10011

Bruce Smith Designs
56 Millward Road
Larkspur, CA 94939

Clodagh
365 First Avenue
New York, NY 10010

Damga Design, Inc.
812 Broadway
New York, NY 10003

D'Aquino Humphreys Interiors
520 Broadway
New York, NY 10012

DuBay and Maire Designs
445 North Wells Street, Suite 200
Chicago, IL 60610

Gwathmey Siegel and Associates Architects
472 10th Avenue
New York, NY 10018

Haverson/Rockwell Architects, PC
106 West 27th Street
New York, NY 10023

Huberman Designs
21 Pond Path
Woodbury, NY 11797

Joan Halperin Interior Design
401 East 80th Street
New York, NY 10021

The Joseph Boggs Studio/Architects
1333 H Street N.W.
The Landmark Building
Washington, DC 20005

Kevin Walz Design
141 Fifth Avenue
New York, NY 10010

Leonard Colchamiro, PC, AIA
227 Fifth Avenue
Brooklyn, NY 11215

Margaret Helfand Architects
32 East 38th Street
New York, NY 10016

Mariette Himes Gomez Associates, Inc.
291 East 78th Street
New York, NY 10021

Melvin Dwork, Inc.
405 East 56th Street
New York, NY 10022

Michael DeSantis
1110 Second Avenue
New York, NY 10022

Michael LaRocca Interiors
150 East 58th Street #3510
New York, NY 10155

Nick Calder Designs
1365 York Avenue Apt. 3K
New York, NY 10022

Noel Jeffrey, Inc.
215 East 58th Street
New York, NY 10022

Ojinaga
Rast, 29 Bjios.
08021 Barcelona, Spain

Ronn Jaffe Associates, Inc.
The Design Studio Building
9204 Harrington
Potomac, MD 20854

Sandra Nunnerley Designs
400 East 55th Street
New York, NY 10022

Scott Bromley Interiors
242 West 27th Street
New York, NY 10001

Thomas Hauser Design, Ltd.
415 West 55th Street
New York, NY 10019

Wolk Design Associates
4265 Braganza Street
Coconut Grove, Fl 33133

INDEX

PHOTOGRAPHERS